The UN Security Council (2006)
Practice and promise
by Edward C. Luck (Columbia University)

The World Intellectual Property Organization (2006)
Resurgence and the development agenda
by Chris May (University of Lancaster)

The North Atlantic Treaty Organization (2007)
The enduring alliance
by Julian Lindley-French (European Union Centre for Security Studies)

The International Monetary Fund (2007)
Politics of conditional lending
by James Raymond Vreeland (Yale University)

The Group of 7/8 (2007)
by Hugo Dobson (University of Sheffield)

The World Economic Forum (2007)
A multi-stakeholder approach to global governance
by Geoffrey Allen Pigman (Bennington College)

The International Committee of the Red Cross (2007)
A neutral humanitarian actor
*by David Forsythe (University of Nebraska) and
Barbara Ann Rieffer-Flanagan (Central Washington University)*

The Organization for Security and Co-operation in Europe (2007)
by David J. Galbreath (University of Aberdeen)

United Nations Conference on Trade and Development (UNCTAD) (2007)
by Ian Taylor (University of St. Andrews) and Karen Smith (University of Stellenbosch)

A Crisis of Global Institutions? (2007)
Multilateralism and international security
by Edward Newman (University of Birmingham)

The World Trade Organization (2007)
Law, economics, and politics
by Bernard Hoekman (World Bank) and Petros Mavroidis (Columbia University)

The African Union (2008)
Challenges of globalization, security and governance
by Samuel M. Makinda (Murdoch University) and F. Wafula Okumu (Institute for Security Studies)

Commonwealth (2008)
Inter- and non-state contributions to global governance
by Timothy M. Shaw (Royal Roads University and University of the West Indies)

The European Union (2008)
by Clive Archer (Manchester Metropolitan University)

The World Bank (2008)
From reconstruction to development to equity
by Katherine Marshall (Georgetown University)

Contemporary Human Rights Ideas
by Bertrand G. Ramcharan (Geneva Graduate Institute of International Studies)

For further information regarding the series, please contact:

Craig Fowlie, Publisher, Politics & International Studies
Taylor & Francis
2 Park Square, Milton Park, Abingdon
Oxford OX14 4RN, UK

+44 (0)207 842 2057 Tel
+44 (0)207 842 2302 Fax

Craig.Fowlie@tandf.co.uk
www.routledge.com

Commonwealth

Inter- and non-state contributions
to global governance

Timothy M. Shaw

Routledge
Taylor & Francis Group

LONDON AND NEW YORK

First published 2008
by Routledge
2 Park Square, Milton Park, Abingdon, Oxon OX14 4RN

Simultaneously published in the USA and Canada
by Routledge
270 Madison Avenue, New York, NY 10016

Routledge is an imprint of the Taylor & Francis Group, an informa business

© 2008 Timothy M. Shaw

Typeset in Times New Roman by
Taylor & Francis Books
Printed and bound in Great Britain by
Antony Rowe Ltd, Chippenham, Wiltshire

British Library Cataloguing in Publication Data
A catalogue record for this book is available from the British Library

Library of Congress Cataloging in Publication Data
Shaw, Timothy M.
    Commonwealth : inter- and nonstate contributions to global
governance / Timothy M. Shaw.
      p. cm. – (Routledge global institutions)
    Includes bibliographical references and index.
     1. International cooperation. 2. Democratization. 3. Globalization.
  I. Title.

JZ1318.S534 2007
341.2–dc22   2007016950

ISBN 978-0-415-35120-1 (hbk)
ISBN 978-0-415-35121-8 (pbk)
ISBN 978-0-203-93732-7 (ebk)

Contents

Illustrations

Foreword

The current volume is the nineteenth in a dynamic series on "global institutions." The series strives (and, based on the volumes published to date, succeeds) to provide readers with definitive guides to the most visible aspects of what we know as "global governance." Remarkable as it may seem, there exist relatively few books that offer in-depth treatments of prominent global bodies and processes, much less an entire series of concise and complementary volumes. Those that do exist are either out of date, inaccessible to the non-specialist reader, or seek to develop a specialized understanding of particular aspects of an institution or process rather than offer an overall account of its functioning. Similarly, existing books have often been written in highly technical language or have been crafted "in-house" and are notoriously self-serving and narrow.

The advent of electronic media has helped by making information, documents, and resolutions of international organizations more widely available, but it has also complicated matters. The growing reliance on the Internet and other electronic methods of finding information about key international organizations and processes has served, ironically, to limit the educational materials to which most readers have ready access—namely, books. Public relations documents, raw data, and loosely refereed websites do not make for intelligent analysis. Official publications compete with a vast amount of electronically available information, much of which is suspect because of its ideological or self-promoting slant. Paradoxically, a growing range of purportedly independent websites offering analyses of the activities of particular organizations has emerged, but one inadvertent consequence has been to frustrate access to basic, authoritative, critical, and well researched texts. The market for such has actually been reduced by the ready availability of varying quality electronic materials.

For those of us who teach, research, and practice in the area, this access to information has been particularly frustrating. We were delighted when Routledge saw the value of a series that bucks this trend and provides key reference points to the most significant global institutions. They are betting that serious students and professionals will want serious analyses. We have assembled a first-rate line-up of authors to address that market. Our intention, then, is to provide one-stop shopping for all readers—students (both undergraduate and postgraduate), interested negotiators, diplomats, practitioners from nongovernmental and intergovernmental organizations, and interested parties alike—seeking information about most prominent institutional aspects of global governance.

The Commonwealth(s)

The Commonwealth is a slightly anachronistic, somewhat hidden, but nevertheless important actor in global governance. As an association of (largely) former British colonies—it began as exclusively so—that spans one-third of the world's population and over a quarter of the UN's member states, the Commonwealth is both a relic of an older, imperial form of global governance as well as a forward-looking (inter- and nongovernmental) institution dedicated to dealing with issues of contemporary concern that firmly locates it within a modern, diffuse, and multi-actor version of global governance. Inevitably, the Commonwealth reflects both these identities. British imperialism serves as the Commonwealth's *raison d'être* for an association of states that comprises the advanced economies of the former metropole (the United Kingdom), Canada, and Australia, along with the largest democracy in the world (India) and the micro states of Nauru and Tuvalu, among others; the Queen remains head of state for 16 of the 53 member states (albeit all are "independent"); and accusations, that the institution has been used to maintain British influence periodically ring out during Commonwealth Heads of Government Meetings (CHOGM), often from those who have, in one way or another, found themselves to be at variance with the institution's core principles.

In reality, the Commonwealth currently has little to do with the imperial heritage from which it emerged. The principles to which its members subscribe, and indeed the willingness of the institution to press issues of international concern particularly at times when to do so is at variance with prevailing orthodoxies, have been among its many strengths. From the outset, the Commonwealth sought to be a voluntary association of nations based on the principle of sovereign equality. At a time when the Cold War raged and states were encouraged to side with one or other of the superpowers (or else declare themselves non-aligned), the institution endorsed the principle of freedom of alignment. Anti-racism, motivated not only by apartheid South Africa's formal system of separation but also the persistence of other forms of informal and latent discrimination, has been a defining principle of the Commonwealth. It has consistently sought to press for fairer terms of trade, correctives to global inequalities in income and wealth, the rule of law, freedom of expression and participatory forms of democracy. These principles and others have been enshrined in the institution's key documents, of which the 1971 Singapore Declaration and the 1991 Harare Declarations are perhaps the most notable.

The Commonwealth prides itself on being one of the very few international organizations that actually sanctions its members for violating the core democratic and human rights principles upon which it is founded. The suspension of Zimbabwe in 2002 for serious irregularities in, and violence during, the presidential election is probably the most well known example of the Commonwealth's collective willingness to sanction its members. Others have also been on the receiving end of such action: Nigeria was suspended in 1995 following, among other things, the execution of activist Ken Saro-Wiwa; Pakistan was suspended in 1999 for the overthrow of a democratically elected government; and, Fiji was suspended in 2001 for election irregularities.

Yet, the Commonwealth is far more than merely an intergovernmental institution in the constellation of global institutions that combine to produce contemporary global governance. It is also a "family" of non-government bodies each working to promote cooperation, peace and understanding among citizens residing in the member states. This family comprises more than 80 associations, ranging from the Association of Commonwealth Universities, the Commonwealth Association of Indigenous Peoples, the Commonwealth Human Rights Initiative, and the Commonwealth's women's network, to the Commonwealth Association of Museums, and the Victoria League for Commonwealth Friendship. Indeed, the reader will discover that the title of the book might well have been *The Commonwealths*!

A book on this unusual body was an obvious addition to a series on Global Institutions and the author an easy choice. We were delighted when Tim Shaw agreed to our request to put a book together on this unique and dynamic institution. Tim's credentials to write this book are second to none. He had just assumed his current post as Professor at Royal Roads University in British Columbia after serving for five years as the Director of the Institute of Commonwealth Studies at the University of London. Indeed, much of his own professional experience as a scholar and visitor has taken place in universities located in the Commonwealth—in Canada, Uganda, South Africa, Nigeria, Zimbabwe (when it was not suspended), Zambia, and the UK—and he did his graduate studies in Uganda and the United States (whose early anti-colonial struggle ironically locates it outside of the traditional Commonwealth). He has written or edited some 40 books and published over 200 journal articles and book chapters on issues related to the Commonwealth, international development, African politics, and international political economy. And, he has served in various capacities in roles related to the work of the Commonwealth, including as Commissioner to the UK Commonwealth Scholarship Commission and Member of the Civil Society Advisory Committee of the Commonwealth Foundation.

We are delighted with the end result and heartily recommend it. It deserves to be studied by all those interested in global governance. As always, comments and suggestions from readers are most welcome.

Thomas G. Weiss, The CUNY Graduate Center, New York, USA
Rorden Wilkinson, University of Manchester, UK
October 2007

Acknowledgments

The welcome challenge to draft this book—on an idiosyncratic yet invaluable, though frequently overlooked, family of inter- and non-state organizations—came from the editors of the Global Institutions series, Tom Weiss and Rorden Wilkinson, in mid-2003 while I was serving as Director of the Institute of Commonwealth Studies at the University of London. I was delighted as well as challenged by the opportunity, though only faintly aware of the demanding twists and turns in the road ahead as analyst, author and editor. The journey was complicated and lengthened as I extended the reach—the conceptual map—of the "Commonwealths" beyond familiar, formal arrangements to more extensive informal interactions and as I relocated half way around the world. I crafted the bulk of this manuscript in the fall of 2006 and spring of 2007 while a faculty member at Royal Roads University in Victoria, British Columbia: a delightful, aesthetic outpost of "empire."

I could not have contemplated this assignment without the encouragement of and contributions from several overlapping analytic networks, some now stretching over four decades, which have been facilitated by new technologies and grants. I liken these to the Olympic "rings" which overlap with each other while also being distinctive: generations of students and colleagues (usually friendly), both professorial and practitioner, in the Commonwealths, development, globalization, governance, international political economy, international relations, and so on, especially in Africa, Europe and North America.

I was particularly pleased by the opportunity to expand analysis of the Commonwealths (plural) by juxtaposing a set of overlapping fields, even if they had not before been so interspersed: Commonwealth studies, development studies, global governance, global and globalization studies, international political economy, international relations, and "new" security studies, and I have appreciated and incorporated inputs both specific and generic from academic and applied practitioners within each of these genres.

In turn, mercifully, I have been saved from myriad errors, misjudgments and embarrassment by Terry Barringer, Richard Bourne, Derek Ingram, David McIntyre, Andrew Williams *et al.* I recognize that they have reservations about my continuing concern with comparative global governance and do not always approve of my pluralization of Commonwealths or globalizations. Some, like Tony Payne, have even suggested that I have invented a new language—Timish!—to facilitate, and possibly obscure, such analysis.

With such invaluable assistance and networks, as well as generosity, I have been able to submit this book in time for it to appear just ahead of the end-2007 Commonwealth summit in Kampala, Uganda. This is most welcome not only because I have been privileged to serve as a member of the Civil Society Advisory Committee to the Commonwealth Foundation, which helps to organize the biennial Commonwealth People's Forum, but also because I was fortunate enough to be a graduate student at Makerere University (then the University of East Africa) in the late 1960s. Given all the subsequent advantages that those three years gave me, I am delighted that we can launch this volume back in the "Pearl of Africa" as Uganda once again aspires to be a center for development on the continent.

Victoria, BC
Spring 2007

Abbreviations

16CCEM	16th Conference of Commonwealth Ministers of Education
ABC	Australia, Britain, Canada
ACU	Association of Commonwealth Universities
AKF	Aga Khan Foundation
AU	African Union
BRICs	Brazil, Russia, India and China (emerging economies)
CBC	Commonwealth Business Council
CF	Commonwealth Foundation
CfCE	Consortium for Commonwealth Education
CFTC	Commonwealth Fund for Technical Cooperation
CGF	Commonwealth Games Federation
CHOGM	Commonwealth Heads of Government Meeting
CHRI	Commonwealth Human Rights Initiative
CJA	Commonwealth Journalists' Association
CLA	Commonwealth Lawyers' Association
CMA	Commonwealth Medical Association
CMAG	Commonwealth Ministerial Action Group
COG	Commonwealth Organizations' Group
COL	Commonwealth of Learning
ComSec	Commonwealth Secretariat
CPA	Commonwealth Parliamentary Association
CPF	Commonwealth Peoples' Forum
CSR	corporate social responsibility
CTO	Commonwealth Telecommunications Organization
CYP	Commonwealth Youth Programme
DAC	Development Assistance Committee (of the OECD)
EG	Expert Group (in ComSec)
EITI	Extractive Industries Transparency Initiative
ESU	English-Speaking Union

EU	European Union
IBSA	India, Brazil and South Africa
ICC	International Cricket Council
ICTs	information and communications technologies
IFIs	international financial institutions
KP	Kimberley Process (to ban conflict diamonds)
MDGs	Millennium Development Goals (UN)
NGO	nongovernmental organization
NICs	newly industrializing countries
OAS	Organization of American States
OECD	Organization for Economic Cooperation and Development
OTs	Overseas Territories (of Britain)
RCS	Royal Commonwealth Society
UN	United Nations
UNDP	United Nations Development Programme

Introduction

Commonwealths in comparative perspective

> Past literature on the Commonwealth has been overwhelmingly descriptive, historical and lacking in theoretical substance. It has also, perhaps like the Commonwealth itself, sought to avoid controversy and has been largely devoid of any strong critical reflection on the organization.
>
> (Ian Taylor)[1]

As a partial response to the above lament, this book seeks to put the English-speaking Commonwealths (plural; i.e. as explained below, non- as well as inter-state agencies and networks) in comparative, conceptual context, with applied as well as analytic relevance. I do so in at least four ways which:

- contrast the inter- and non-governmental Commonwealths, as the former, "official" dimension has held most analytic and policy attention over the years despite the "unofficial" being the more dynamic and expansive, a dominant theme of this book as outlined in Chapter 1;
- consider the contribution, if any, of both "sides" of the Commonwealths to the analysis and practice of "global governance" (see especially Chapters 3 and 6);
- compare the Commonwealths to other established global and regional agencies, from the United Nations (UN) and international financial institutions (IFI) "systems" to the African Union (AU), European Union (EU) and Organization of American States (OAS), for example; and, finally, in particular,
- juxtapose the anglophone Commonwealth, which has its roots in the British empire (see Chapter 2) with parallel ex-imperial Commonwealths, notably *la francophonie* and the lusophone, Russian, Spanish and even "Nordic" and Islamic Commonwealths as indicated in the next chapter.

This analysis is distinctive because it deliberately pluralizes "Commonwealths"—however awkward and unfamiliar a term—to indicate that these post-colonial networks are not only intergovernmental but also non-state, or "non-official" institutions. Unusually, I also stretch the purview of the Commonwealths' networks to organizations and interactions which are only loosely connected, such as civil societies and multinational corporations whose activities are primarily located in the Commonwealths. Such plurality not only recognizes the contribution, even creativity, of myriad non-state actors. It is also historically rooted or reflective as several major nongovernmental agencies preceded the formal establishment of the Commonwealth Secretariat as an intergovernmental organization in the mid-1960s.

Such a sequence is not characteristic of international communities. Typically, non-state connections succeed rather than precede the formal inter-state. Even in the case of the UN, while most of its agencies, like the UN Development Programme, are post-1945, it did inherit the International Labor Organization and the World Health Organization in Geneva from the defunct League of Nations. By contrast, the IFIs created almost all of their associated agencies after their Bretton Woods conception, as did the AU and EU, for example. And all the other non-anglophone Commonwealth-type institutions identified in Chapter 1 were established and have remained as essentially intergovernmental arrangements only, unlike the anglophone networks with their distinctive and dynamic nongovernmental dimensions.

Similarly, the concept of "global governance" constitutes a contemporary extension and elaboration of the earlier, established notions of international organization and international law. But, in parallel to the plural Commonwealths, it has come to embrace and advance non- as well as inter-state actors and associations. Indeed, increasingly, such nongovernmental agencies and networks are recognized to be as, if not more, salient than the intergovernmental as sources of the ideas which animate contemporary international relations and coalitions, as reflected in the list of "Commonwealth Plus" websites following the select annotated bibliography at the end of the book.[2] Such governance can take place at regional in addition to global levels, and it increasingly recognizes and advances as well as incorporates a diversity of actors and issues. So catalysts for global governance can now be civil societies or private corporations, think tanks or assorted media as indicated in the second half of this volume. But they almost all need a variety of heterogeneous institutions, including the inter-state, to create and sustain winning coalitions around contemporary "global" issues like blood diamonds, child soldiers, development, gender, global warming, fundamentalisms, land-mines or small arms.[3]

Despite constituting the second most extensive international organization of communities after the universal UN system, as indicated by the opening citation from Ian Taylor, the Commonwealths have been largely ignored in the burgeoning field of studies of such contemporary global governance.[4] This volume seeks to correct this neglect by describing and analyzing the contributions and limitations of the Commonwealth Secretariat and Foundation along with the myriad professional associations and civil society networks rooted in and related to them. Moreover, it goes beyond these relatively familiar networks to suggest that the Commonwealths have both facilitated and benefited from myriad Commonwealth Plus organizations in the communications, cultural, diasporic, educational, media and private sectors: the overlooked overlap or extrapolation between anglophone Commonwealths and anglophone globalization (see Chapters 4 to 6 below).

The former—Secretariat or ComSec—is the intergovernmental agency which serves the Commonwealth's current (mid-2007) 53 member states. By contrast, the latter—Foundation—is the very modest office to advance two distinct but broadly compatible nongovernmental dimensions of the Commonwealth community: the frequently well established "professional associations," some of which pre-date ComSec, and the relatively recent civil society organizations, typically NGOs or INGOs ((international) nongovernmental organizations). The latter are becoming recognized and reflected in its latest institutional innovation, an NGO-centric Civil Society Advisory Committee, treated in the first chapter.

In terms of the former type connected to the Foundation—professional associations—the Commonwealths' "extended family" includes, for example, the well established Association of Commonwealth Universities (ACU) of some 500 universities; Commonwealth Parliamentary Association (CPA) (170 parliaments/assemblies with 15,000 members); Commonwealth Press Union, the first to be founded—in 1909—to secure press freedom; and Commonwealth Games (over 70 "national" and 6–7,000 individual participants), all of which preceded the formal establishment of ComSec and Foundation. And it now reaches to the relatively recent (INGO-oriented) Commonwealth Human Rights Initiative (CHRI) (founded by five compatible Commonwealth professional associations in 1987) and onto global networks around Commonwealth literatures and related cultural connections including diasporas (see Appendix 3 for a listing of major Commonwealth inter- and nongovernmental organizations).

Table 1.1 Key indicators on the Millennium Development Goals

	Total population, '000s, 2004	GNI per capita, US$, 2004	GDP per capita growth, % p.a., 1990–2004	Net primary enrolment ratio, %, 2000–5	Adult literacy rate, %, 2000–5	Life expectancy, years, 2004	Infant mortality, per 1,000, 2004	Percentage of population living with HIV/AIDS, 2005	PCs per 1,000 people, 2004–5
Antigua and Barbuda	81	9,480	1.6			72	11		
Australia	19,942	27,070	2.5	96		81	5	0.08	689
The Bahamas	319	15,800		84		70	10	2.11	
Bangladesh	139,215	440	3.1	84		63	56	0.01	12
Barbados	269	9,270		97		75	10	1.00	149
Belize	264	3,940	2.2	95		72	32	1.37	135
Botswana	1,769	4,360	2.9	82	81	35	84	15.30	45
Brunei Darussalam	366	24,100			93	77	8		85
Cameroon	16,038	810	0.4	79	68	46	87	3.12	10
Canada	31,958	28,310	2.3	99		80	5	0.19	698
Cyprus	826	16,510	3.1	96	97	79	5		309
Dominica	79	3,670	1.1	88		75	13		182
Fiji Islands	841	2,720	1.7	96		68	16		52
The Gambia	1,478	280	0.2	53	58	56	89	1.32	16
Ghana	21,664	380	1.9	65		57	68	1.45	5
Grenada	102	3,750	2.3	84		65	18		157
Guyana	750	1,020	3.3	97		64	48	1.60	39
India	1,087,124	620	4.1	76	61	64	62	0.52	15
Jamaica	2,639	3,300	0.0	91	80	71	17	0.94	62
Kenya	33,467	480	-0.6	76	74	48	79	3.79	10
Kiribati	97	970	2.5	97		62	49		12
Lesotho	1,798	730	2.3	65	82	35	61	15.04	
Malawi	12,608	160	0.9	82	64	40	110	7.30	2
Malaysia	24,894	4,520	3.3	93	89	73	10	0.27	192

Country									
Maldives	321	2,410	4.6	90	96	67	35		110
Malta	400	12,050	3.0	94	88	79	5		166
Mauritius	1,233	4,640	3.9	95	84	72	14	0.33	162
Mozambique	19,424	270	4.8	60		42	104	9.09	6
Namibia	2,009	2,380	0.9	74	85	47	47	11.32	109
Nauru	13	6,424				63	25		
New Zealand	3,989	19,990	2.1	99		79	5	0.03	482
Nigeria	128,709	430	0.2	60	50	43	101	2.20	7
Pakistan	154,794	600	1.1	56	57	63	80	0.05	4
Papua New Guinea	5,772	560	0.0			56	68	1.02	63
St.Kitts-Nevis	42	7,600	2.9	94		72	18		261
St.Lucia	159	4,180	0.3	98		73	13		163
St.Vincent & the Grenadines	118	3,400	1.9	94		71	18		132
Samoa	184	1,840	2.2	90	92	71	25		7
Seychelles	80	8,190	1.7	96	35	72	12	0.87	198
Sierra Leone	5,336	210	-2.5	41	93	41	165	0.13	
Singapore	4,273	24,760	3.5			79	3		622
Solomon Islands	466	560	-2.6	80		63	34		46
South Africa	47,208	3,630	0.4	89	82	47	54	11.60	84
Sri Lanka	20,570	1,010	3.3	99	91	74	12	0.02	27
Swaziland	1,034	1,660	0.2	77	80	31	108	21.32	33
Tonga	102	1,860	2.0	91	99	72	20		50
Trinidad and Tobago	1,301	8,730	3.5	92		70	18	2.07	79
Tuvalu	10					68	36		
Uganda	27,821	250	3.8	87	67	48	80	3.47	9
United Kingdom	59,479	33,630	2.5	99		79	5	0.11	600
United Republic of Tanzania*	37,627	320	1.3	73	69	46	78	3.65	7
Vanuatu	207	1,390	-0.8	94	74	69	32		14
Zambia	11,479	400	-0.6	57	68	38	102	9.43	10

Note: * GNI data for mainland Tanzania only

1 Antigua and Barbuda
2 Australia
3 The Bahamas
4 Bangladesh
5 Barbados
6 Belize
7 Botswana
8 Brunei Darussalam
9 Cameroon
10 Canada
11 Cyprus
12 Dominica
13 Fiji Islands (suspended from the councils of the Commonwealth in December 2006)
14 The Gambia
15 Ghana
16 Grenada
17 Guyana
18 India
19 Jamaica
20 Kenya
21 Kiribati
22 Lesotho
23 Malawi
24 Malaysia
25 Maldives
26 Malta
27 Mauritius
28 Mozambique
29 Namibia
30 Nauru (special member)
31 New Zealand
32 Nigeria
33 Pakistan
34 Papua New Guinea
35 St Kitts and Nevis
36 St Lucia
37 St Vincent and the Grenadines
38 Samoa
39 Seychelles
40 Sierra Leone
41 Singapore
42 Solomon Islands
43 South Africa
44 Sri Lanka
45 Swaziland
46 Tonga
47 Trinidad and Tobago
48 Tuvalu
49 Uganda
50 United Kingdom
51 United Republic of Tanzania
52 Vanuatu
53 Zambia

Map I.1 Commonwealth map.

Map source: Commonwealth Secretariat/Maps-in-Minutes™

The designations and the presentation of material on this map, based on UN practice, do not imply the expression of any opinion whatsoever on the part of the Commonwealth Secretariat or of the publishers concerning the legal status of any country, territory or area, or of its authorities, or concerning the delimitation of its frontiers or boundaries.

And given my own recognition or inclusion of extra- or non-Commonwealth agencies within my more comprehensive analytic framework, as explained and elaborated in the chapters which follow below, I would extend the latter type beyond recognized inter- and non-state institutions like the Commonwealth Games Federation (CGF) of over 70 members to global Commonwealth-centric organizations like, say, the International Cricket Council (ICC) and its World Cup (in South Africa in 2003 and the West Indies in 2007 and on to South Asia in 2011) or the International Rugby Board and its Rugby World Cup hosted by the "new" South Africa in 1995 (see Chapter 5 below).

Furthermore, then, given interrelated factors of

- democratic criteria;
- English as the lingua franca of globalization; and
- migrations and diasporas (as well as exclusion of the United States),

I would push the contributions and claims of the Commonwealths even further, beyond Commonwealth Secretariat, Foundation and Associations, however controversial or original the analytic perspective. Arguably, they have all benefited from and contributed to contemporary "globalization," in part as it is inseparable from the largely anglophone worlds of business, communications, finance, higher education, technology, etc. I characterize such features as Commonwealth Plus, on which more below. So the Commonwealths' traditions of English "democratic" cultures and processes and cosmopolitan education and language can be treated as contributing factors to migrations and diasporas. I take all to be aspects of the globalization of economy and society (see Chapters 4 and 5 below).

No other ex-imperial organization has benefited from such a coincidence. Typically, old empires decline without such a continuing, let alone burgeoning, legacy. In the case of today's Commonwealths, their global impact is in part a function of one of the ex-colonies which never joined but rather was the first to rebel against the British crown—the United States. It became the sole global superpower in the 1990s, at least for a while. Ironically, notwithstanding America's aversion to the British empire, as indicated in Chapter 6, a small conservative group of "yanks" with traditional "New England" inclinations continues to advocate an "anglosphere" of transatlantic countries plus the scattered old "white" Dominions,[5] a not uncontroversial aspiration.[6]

To anticipate Ian Taylor's further lament at the end as well as start of this introduction, the contemporary Commonwealths can also be treated as cases of "new multilateralisms," with the adjective "new" relating to both new actors and new issues. The concept reflects the identification of and response to a set of new global issues by a heterogeneous set of interests, not just a variety of states. The range of proliferating international issues stretches from global warming to global epidemics, global brands to the global drugs trade. Both Commonwealths and such multilateralisms today involve not only states but also non-state actors, both civil society and private sector. Together, these two types of non-state actors contribute to "triangular" relations (see Figure I.1 below) both cooperative and competitive, of state and non-state institutions: the basis of such current heterogeneous multilateralisms.

Reflective of prevailing ideas about national development in the initial post-colonial period—the era of so-called "state socialism"—the private sector was rather overlooked until the end of the century inside and outside the Commonwealths, with the Commonwealth Business Council (CBC) not being created until 1997. Nevertheless, the "Commonwealth factor" has advanced trade and other economic relations within the anglophone world of countries and companies, especially in some sectors as indicated below. Arguably, this advances globalization, especially as the latter has been reinforced by "newly industrializing countries" (NICs) like Singapore and now "emerging economies" like India, both well established Commonwealth members. And today the CBC has a very busy schedule of events throughout the Commonwealth, especially around the biennial Commonwealth Heads of Government Meetings (CHOGMs) and the annual fall meetings of ministers of finance. Its 200 member companies span the Commonwealth and its management board includes captains of industry from major countries and companies.

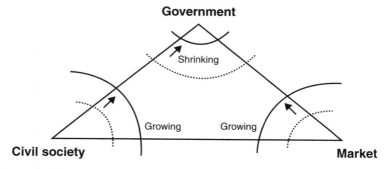

Figure I.1 Commonwealth governance triangle.

Meanwhile, conversely, as not unimportant features of a world of more than 200 states, the Commonwealths increasingly transcend their imperial inheritance from and dependence on the white Dominions—the ABC (Australia, Britain and Canada of Commonwealth nomenclature (including New Zealand, of course))—all of which are increasingly multi-cultural and multi-racial. Instead, they now include a few NICs (i.e. Singapore with Malaysia unquestionably a near-NIC and Mauritius an aspiring one) and emerging economies or BRICs (India having along with China the biggest population in the world and now both of them booming economically) as well as several "fragile states" and developing islands. And as Richard Bourne notes of the then G-54, "half have populations of less than 1.5 million, a majority are islands and only six are entirely landlocked … over half the citizens of the G-54 live in India, and nearly two-thirds live in South Asia."[7]

By contrast to almost all other international organizations, half a dozen members have been suspended from intergovernmental Councils, especially the biannual CHOGM summit—Fiji was again at end-2006 for the second or third time to be readmitted after resuming democratic norms. And several member states, particularly in Africa, have emerged at the end of the twentieth century from difficult "transitions"; e.g. Mozambique, South Africa and Uganda. Such diversity, along with shifts in national rankings—Singapore now has a higher per capita income than New Zealand while incomes in Mauritius and Botswana are higher than those of Malaysia and South Africa—constitute further reasons for focusing on the Commonwealths in a series on comparative

Table I.2   Human Development Indicators for Commonwealth states

High	Antigua and Barbuda, Australia, Bahamas, Barbados, Brunei, Canada, Cyprus, Malaysia, Malta, Mauritius, New Zealand, St. Kitts-Nevis, Seychelles, Singapore, Tonga, Trinidad and Tobago, UK (17)
Medium	Bangladesh, Belize, Botswana, Cameroon, Dominica, Fiji, Ghana, Grenada, Guyana, India, Jamaica, Maldives, Namibia, Pakistan, Papua New Guinea, St. Lucia, Samoa, Solomon Islands, South Africa, Sri Lanka, Swaziland, Uganda, Vanuatu (23)
Low	Gambia, Kenya, Lesotho, Malawi, Mozambique, Nigeria, Sierra Leone, Tanzania, Zambia (9)

Source: UNDP, *Human Development Report 2006*, 283, 286 and 413.

Notes:
First in Commonwealth: Australia (no. 3 globally with HDI value of 0.957); last in Commonwealth: Sierra Leone (no. 176 globally with HDI value of 0.335).

global institutions at start of the twenty-first century. Why have they been previously disregarded in comparative studies of global governance?

The emergence of the global governance perspective since the end of the Cold War parallels the evolution of the Commonwealths: both are increasingly established and recognized. The former consists of analysis and advocacy by myriad heterogeneous actors—inter- and non-state alike—who seek to advance global development and security such as via global coalitions against land-mines or "blood diamonds." And the latter embrace an extensive network of formally recognized or accredited and informally connected associations and arrangements; these tend to have "fuzzy" edges as memberships vary from less to more than 53 states. Both increasingly incorporate a range of non-state as well as intergovernmental institutions, notably NGOs and MNCs. While historically these have been antagonistically inclined, in recent years they have come to identify and recognize some mutual interests in "partnerships" over a range of global issues like communications, diversity, gender, HIV/AIDS, labor, etc. I treat the UN Global Compact and its Commonwealth parallels in Chapter 5 below.

Arguably, the Commonwealths were in the vanguard of moves to open up inter-state organizations to non-state participation toward the end of the last century in part, as already noted above, nongovernmental institutions and networks often preceded the formal establishment of the Secretariat at Marlborough House in London. While relations between Commonwealth governments and agencies and Commonwealth civil societies and multinational corporations are not always easy or harmonious, they did anticipate parallels in the IFIs; e.g. the Global Development Network (GDN) and the UN Global Compact, both products of the end of the Cold War.[8] Indeed, the Commonwealths are very decentralized so that no one agency regulates the use of the Commonwealth "logo" or "brand." Thus the connection can be misused or misleading as some so-called "Commonwealth" institutions are at best semi-detached.

Characteristic of such new multilateralisms are, then, the Ottawa and Kimberley Processes around land-mines and conflict diamonds, respectively. But many other "strategic alliances" of a diverse and fluid range of actors and interests have begun to emerge around myriad global issues and strategic sectors such as corruption, diasporas, disasters, ecology, energy, health, security, technology, etc., as well as notable disappointments as over child soldiers or small arms. But such "enlightened" multilateralisms continue to bump up against resilient US unilateralism, which retains a *de facto* veto, at least at the global level. When and where have the Commonwealths contributed to or obstructed such global development? Such questions are rarely formulated let alone posed, further symbols of oversight or neglect.

Despite their venerable imperial origins (see Chapter 2), the formal institutions of the Commonwealths are younger than those of the UN and IFI systems; both Secretariat and Foundation marked just four decades in 2005[9] whereas the UN and IFIs turned 60. And the CBC is the Johnny-come-lately, having not been established until toward the end of the 1990s even though Australian, British, Canadian, South African and Indian global companies go back centuries, especially those in "colonial" sectors like commodities, energy, minerals and textiles. However, the organizational or political cultures of all of them have their roots in the British empire, especially its inter- and post-war iterations and evolutions. Their unofficial policy journal *Round Table* will celebrate its centenary in 2010 (see Chapter 4 below), the CPU its own the previous year in 2009 and the CPA a year later in 2011; likewise the ACU will turn a hundred in 2013; i.e. they were all established before World War I. And the Commonwealth Games commenced in Canada between the wars: in 1930.

As suggested in the opening chapter below, the organizational culture of the Commonwealths thus has a rather different, more collaborative, tone from the somewhat adversarial, zero-sum character of those in the UN and IFIs: more informal and familial. In part this reflects the legacy of extended imperial gatherings in country retreats in Britain until the summits began to circulate throughout the world in 1971, initially around the larger and more affluent member states, first in Singapore. And in part it reflects the relative unimportance and impecunity of the organization compared to the visibility of the UN and the affluence of the IFIs. It does not include today's hegemon as a member and no-one holds a veto so all votes or opinions are formally equal. The recurrent biennial sequence of events leading toward the CHOGM is distinct from annual UN assemblies and IFI meetings or occasional issue-specific summits, whether debt relief or MDGs. Yet it is within such relaxed, non-threatening environments that innovative responses can be considered for novel global issues like racism toward the end of the twentieth century and fundamentalisms in the twenty-first: the Commonwealths as networks or Commonwealth Plus. Following David Armstrong,[10] I treat the Commonwealths as distinctive networks of heterogeneous actors in Chapter 4 below.

This book proceeds from conceptual (Chapter 1) and historical (Chapter 2) overviews to chapters on contemporary human development, human rights and human security (Chapter 3) and the range of Commonwealth Plus contributions to the analysis and practice of multiple forms of globalization (Chapters 4 and 5), concluding with a more speculative preview of possible futures for both inter- and non-state Commonwealths (Chapter 6). These reflect and reinforce the distinctiveness of the Commonwealths *vis-à-vis* other international organizations or forms of global governance.

Symptomatically, official intergovernmental exchanges in the Commonwealth occur amongst High Commissioners based in High Commissions rather than ambassadors from embassies. And while Commonwealth High Commissioners in London do double duty, by also representing member states in Commonwealth deliberations around the Secretariat, especially in the run-up to biennial summits, they are not so formally accredited, unlike ambassadors to the UN in New York or Geneva. Nevertheless, they all participate in regular Commonwealth events, such as annual Commonwealth Day and Lecture, biennial pre-CHOGM preparations, etc. Those whose states are members (some 46 out of 53) are also represented on the Board of the Foundation, so also advancing the non-official Commonwealth nexus as well.

The extended Commonwealth "family" can also at times include another two score very small territories who have status in affiliated agencies like the CGF and CPA. The heterogeneous set of Australian, British and New Zealand Associated Countries, External and Overseas Territories are concentrated in the Caribbean, South Pacific and South Atlantic. According to Green, "The peoples of these states are regarded as part of the Commonwealth family. Their numbers total about 223,600 people."[11]

As indicated in the concluding Chapter 6, there are several eligible states, like Ireland and the United States, who remain outside the nexus: "honorary" Commonwealth members even if their "republican" imperatives so deny. If the London Declaration had been a mere year earlier, then Ireland or Myanmar might have remained in membership. However, Eire might yet join once the Northern Ireland "troubles" are fully resolved in a sustainable manner. Ireland withdrew from the Commonwealths ahead of the London Declaration which would have extended its established connection. There are others who meet some but not all criteria, like Myanmar and the Sudan. And then there are others who have been knocking on the door for some time even though they lack most associational or democratic or historic criteria, from Rwanda to Yemen. In late 2006, the Secretariat established a group, chaired by ex-Jamaican prime minister P. J. Patterson, to consider criteria and candidates once again in the run-up to CHOGM in Uganda at end-2007. It is being advised by an eminent student of the Commonwealths, Professor David McIntyre.

The generic global governance perspective has evolved over the last one or two decades out of established state-centric international law and international organization and onto analysis of and advocacy by myriad, heterogeneous actors who seek to advance global development and security. It reflects and advances a world "community" of over 200 very unequal states—as indicated above, the 50 plus members of the Commonwealths constitute a shifting hierarchy—in which a multitude of large and small NGOs and MNCs are increasingly active and influential, as symbolized by the World Social Forum and World Economic Forum, respectively.[12] As indicated in my opening and concluding chapters below, such an approach has been defined and refined, advanced and revised by a new generation of analysts around global institutions and networks, from the co-editors of this series on Global Institutions, Thomas G. Weiss and Rorden Wilkinson, to Margaret Keck and Kathryn Sikkink, and Andrew Cooper.[13]

I hope, as suggested in the concluding chapter, that this extended essay will contribute another, overlooked case of global governance with analytic and applied relevance, both presently and into the future. It may also augment proliferating programs and courses on global studies now emerging in several social sciences, paralleling those already established in international development studies (IDS) or Commonwealth studies (see Chapter 4 below). Symptomatic of the growing recognition of this interdisciplinary field are professional associations and academic journals: Global Studies Association and Globalization Studies Network on the one hand and *Global Governance* and *Globalizations* on the other. I return to the Commonwealths and Commonwealth, Development and Global Studies in Chapter 4 below.

As already anticipated five years ago, echoing and underlining his opening citation, Ian Taylor regretted that "The Commonwealth as an intergovernmental organization has not been studied with any reference to the growing literature on multilateralism."[14] This book seeks to rectify this oversight, appropriately for a title in a comprehensive series on global institutions. Its thesis is that the Commonwealths do have something to contribute to global governance at the start of the new millennium in both analysis and practice, even if the rest of the world, including almost all the academy, has yet to so notice.

Unlike the relatively established literature which focuses on ComSec—essentially post-colonial diplomatic history[15]—this essay juxtaposes approaches and insights from a set of overlapping approaches or assumptions which together advance or reinforce the embryonic global governance framework: from more familiar or generic international law, international organization, international political economy and international relations to less familiar or more distinctive Commonwealth, development, global, globalization and security studies. Appropriately, as the Commonwealths are different, so approaches to their analysis will embody their own distinctive as well as familiar dimensions.

Thus this book has two interrelated purposes. First, to propose insights into the expanded concept of Commonwealths—beyond the familiar, formal inter- and non-state to the more informal corporate, cultural and social. And, second, to thereby present another revised or extended conceptual framework to advance comparative case studies of myriad heterogeneous forms of global governance in the new century. Its first half, Chapters 1 to 3, present overviews of its genesis and four decades of history, up to contemporary debates around the latest summits in Malta and Kampala. The second half—Chapters 4 to 6—stretches the notion of Commonwealths beyond the non-state as well as inter-state toward more informal civil society, cultural, educational, economic and sports networks, increasingly including the more controversial notions of diasporas, faiths and security.

1 Commonwealth(s)—inter- and non-state

How compatible?

> Global governance implies a wide and seemingly ever-growing range of actors in every domain. Global economic and social affairs have traditionally been viewed as embracing primarily intergovernmental relationships, but increasingly they must be framed in comprehensive enough terms to embrace local and international NGOs, grassroots and citizens' movements, multinational corporations and the global capital market.
>
> (Thomas G. Weiss)[1]

> Because of the very nature of the current international community, following the collapse of the Soviet bloc and the emergence of new dynamics in the global order (or disorder?) ... now is the time for new forms of diplomacy and global strategies. In an extraordinary way, it is almost as if the Commonwealth has leapt in utility from past to future. It is a non-exclusive transnational organization whose time has probably come.
>
> (Deryck Schreuder)[2]

The current Commonwealths of countries and communities, civil societies and multinational companies are increasingly diverse despite commonalities of history and language, perspectives and values. This initial chapter presents an overview of these diversities which have generated a distinctive political culture within the extended family. In turn, this informs the character of multilateral diplomacy around the Commonwealths: a novel version of public diplomacy given the relative influence of their non-state agencies. The chapter concludes by examining the impact of Commonwealth groupings on several regional organizations and by contrasting anglophone with other Commonwealth communities, so comparing their respective contributions to contemporary global governance.

Today's Commonwealths are dominated by middle powers and small states (see Table I.1) and so span many international divides, especially North-South, big-small, continental-island. They do so by being active around a growing range of contemporary issues reflective of the complexities and diversities of the twenty-first century. As suggested already in the Introduction, new multilateralisms of mixed actor coalitions around the Commonwealths, which advance responses to child soldiers, conflict diamonds, forced migrations, small arms, etc., may yet come to be regarded as both invaluable and worthy of emulation. These may come to be seen as a distinctive form of "Commonwealth governance" as elaborated below.

How can what Richard Bourne calls the G-54[3] (now strictly, post-Zimbabwe, the G-53) (for dates of formal joining see Appendix 1) cohere in the new millennium, and so impact the other 150 or so states in today's global society, especially given fissiparous pressures post-9/11 (twin tower and other terrorist attacks on New York and Washington) and 7/7 (terrorist attacks on London underground trains and buses)?

Here I argue that it is their very heterogeneity as well as similarities that unites the contemporary Commonwealths and enables them to communicate and cooperate when other better established and better funded global organizations are increasingly problematic. As Mills and Stremlau have asserted: "The Commonwealth has a number of strengths, among them the very fact that its varied membership, commonalities and trans-regional nature prevent it from becoming a vehicle for any narrow interest or fleetingly fashionable ideology."[4] I also suggest in Chapter 5 that it is the multiple "extra-official" or non-institutional features of the Commonwealths like culture, language and literature, media and sports—Commonwealth Plus—which enable the Secretariat and Foundation to be able to at least make a claim to be influential.

In short, despite being both overlooked and undramatic, the Commonwealths may yet prove to be an anchor that the world community needs to advance human development, human rights and human security in the first decades of the twenty-first century (see Chapter 3 below) against prevailing rhetoric about national security and fundamentalist terrorists. As David McIntyre notes, the Commonwealth is "not a large player as an international entity" yet it has come to have salience in a trio of issue areas where it can leverage its extensive extra-Commonwealth networks: "These three themes—globalization, the vulnerability of small states and the importance of regional organizations—mark the main features of the international environment in which the Commonwealth has to find its niche."[5]

In the preceding Introduction, I lamented the lack of attention paid to the Commonwealths in the burgeoning global governance literature, which is beginning to supersede the more established, state-centric international law and international organization genres. Here I go further to suggest that there is a rather distinctive version of governance being developed within the Commonwealths' nexus: Commonwealth governance. This is distinguished by the particular combination of inter- and non-state actors and issues found in today's Commonwealths. These are different from those already analyzed elsewhere, including in the Global Institutions series, in the more familiar and recognized UN and IFI systems.[6]

Their distinctiveness is best captured graphically in a "governance triangle" presented in a Commonwealth Foundation report on "Citizens and Governance: civil society in the new millennium" (see Figure I.1) which suggests that the established, "top," state corner is shrinking while newer, "bottom" corners of civil society and private sector are growing. This general trend toward economic and political "liberalization" at all levels—from local through national and regional to global—is related to both globalization and privatization; i.e. "structural adjustment" or "neo-liberalism." Relations along all three sides of the governance triangle at all levels are characterized by both cooperation and conflict, with the horizontal side no longer necessarily being characterized by the latter rather than the former. Despite lingering assumptions to the contrary, NGOs and MNCs are increasingly collaborating over mutual interests, encouraged by Commonwealth Foundation and Commonwealth Business Council deliberations and broader global pressures towards strategic alliances in sectors like fisheries, forestry, mining, etc.

The present book suggests then that there is an emerging, distinctive form of Commonwealth governance which seeks to advance cooperation between civil society and the multinational corporation, state and international organization. This aspiration is particularly apparent in the latest Commonwealth Expert Group report chaired by India's present prime minister, Manmohan Singh, as articulated and analyzed in the final chapter.

I now turn to the Commonwealths' diversities before treating their distinctive political culture and public diplomacy. The second part of this chapter identifies other, non-anglophone, Commonwealths and treats contributions from the anglophone Commonwealths to contemporary regionalisms before returning to the possibility of a distinctive Commonwealth governance.

Membership diversities, both inter- and non-state

As indicated below, the Commonwealths may be concentrated geographically in Africa, Australasia, Caribbean, South Asia and the South

Pacific, but they are increasingly diverse in memberships at both inter- and non-state levels, reflective of a changing world of states, corporations and civil societies.

In terms of the intergovernmental Secretariat, member states span the emerging "three worlds" of first, Organization for Economic Cooperation and Development (OECD)/EU; second, NICs and now emerging economies centered on the BRICs; and third, fragile states (see Chapter 4 below and Table I.1).

According to UNDP Human Development Index (HDI) criteria, in mid-decade (see Table I.2), the Commonwealths include 17 states with "high human development" from the ABCs (ABC and New Zealand in the top twenty list of HDI 2006) through Singapore (number 25 between New Zealand and Cyprus, Barbados and Malta) (NB Brunei, Seychelles and St. Kitts-Nevis now all between numbers 30 and 50 in the annual *Human Development Report* (*HDR*); 23 in the medium category including India (number 125 (China is number 81); and 9 in the low group down to Sierra Leone (second to last overall at number 176, just below Mozambique, Malawi, Tanzania and Zambia), including the "Africanization" of the South Pacific as in recent instabilities in the Solomons and Papua.

And according to World Bank data on national incomes (see Table I.1), the Commonwealths include 10 "high income" states (the ABCs and some affluent islands), 13 "upper-middle income" (mainly Caribbean islands, but also Botswana, Malaysia and South Africa), another 13 "lower-middle income" (mainly small states) and 15 "low income" states (mainly Africa, South Asia, including India, and South Pacific).

In turn, companies, who are members of the CBC, can claim to gain from the Commonwealth factor, including major Australian (BHPBilliton and News Corp) and British (Barclays and Shell) as well as Indian (Bajaj, Infosys and Tata) and South African (Anglo American, Johnnic and SABMiller) multinationals. And the Foundation's network stretches from major INGOs like Oxfam and AKF to miniscule indigenous NGOs and grassroots activists (on economic or corporate and civil society as well as cultural and educational Commonwealths see Chapter 5 below).

Conversely, Commonwealth civil society groups also benefit from a Commonwealth factor as does business, even if their gains are not in efficiency or profitability but rather in familiarity and ease of communication, as is apparent in anglophone global networks like Civicus or Third World Network.

Similarly, the CPA includes very large and very small national (Anguilla, Antigua and Barbuda, Nauru, Turks and Caicos, and

Tuvalu) and provincial or state (Nunavut or Yukon versus Uttar Pradesh) assemblies along with OTs like Alderney and St. Helena, as well as the largest and smallest democratic federations in the world: India and St. Kitts-Nevis. The former, India, contains the largest national and state or provincial assemblies anywhere: national Lok Sabha of 545 seats and Uttar Pradesh Legislative Assembly of some 404. Likewise, the Commonwealth Games Federation has a few very large national delegations but also includes some 20 participants who are not Commonwealth member states. And the ACU has mega-universities as members, including federal universities like London and the West Indies (which initially was a branch of London along with Ibadan, Legon and Makerere) in addition to very small schools like Fourah Bay in Sierra Leone and Uganda Martyrs University. It also includes universities who joined when their states were inside the Commonwealth, such as the Universities of Hong Kong and of Zimbabwe, but who continue to pay membership fees. Such fuzzy borders may give these major non-state institutions distinctive identities and roles. If Commonwealth membership is salient for small independent states, such connections may be even more important for very small dependent territories (for more on such diverse state and non-state memberships see Chapter 5 below).

David McIntyre notes that "a trio of influential bodies ... evolved from empire organizations dating from before the 1914–18 war":[7] ACU, CPA and CPU. They have long since been decolonized along with the nongovernmental organization and their lingering special status is being challenged by a set of dynamic post-colonial non-state institutions. To cite McIntyre again: "A virtual explosion in the professional organizations ... began in the 1960s."[8]

Distinctive political culture

The Commonwealths as a range of global agencies display a different "political culture" to better known and funded international organizations like the UN or the IFIs; i.e. IBRD and IMF. In part, this is because they have not to date treated traditional "national" or global security. And in part, it is a function of membership: no US, no EU (just a trio out of 27 member states) and only one of the four BRICs: India. Furthermore, there is no veto, so the voice of the most populous member—India (1.1 billion)—is the same as that of the smallest: Tuvalu (11,000 people).

But in reality there is no voting, not even over whether to suspend an offending member state or regime, just debate and consensus, however elusive, as it was over apartheid in the 1970s and 1980s and again over the fraught issue of Zimbabwe. Indeed, in intra-Commonwealth deliberations, distinctions between officials from member states and those from Secretariat or Foundation networks are marginal; a "family" environment usually prevails in which good ideas are the currency rather than formal status of origin. As Alison Duxbury suggests, "The Commonwealth as an association of over 1.5 billion people, with disparate cultural and ethnic backgrounds, has (been able to) use the human rights debate to reaffirm its role as an international organization."[9]

The Commonwealths may lack the prestige and visibility of the New York, Geneva and Vienna UN and Washington, D.C. IFI behemoths, who can cajole at least sub-contracting NGOs into colla-boration. But, in turn, the Commonwealths also escape the high expectations, let alone the degree of bureaucratization, that the UN and IFI systems generate. The ongoing UN Intellectual History Pro-ject (UNIHP) and the UNDP chronology serve to evaluate the con-tribution of the multilateral UN system over six decades to global peace and development.[10] Similarly, there are histories of the more bilateral Canadian International Development Research Center (IDRC) and British Department for International Development (DFID) under way. Regrettably and somewhat surprisingly, the Commonwealths presently lack their own intellectual history despite being able to claim some responsibility for post-war decolonization, development and multilateralism.

The histories of the Commonwealths overlap with those of the British empire, which have been revived as well as romanticized of late. But the decolonization process, which began to be conceived and dis-cussed between the wars, at least within Fabian Society and Labour Party circles, but only effected after 1945, have not received the attention they deserve as major catalysts for multilateral institutions like the UN and IFIs let alone the seeds of the contemporary Com-monwealths. The national and regional case studies in British Docu-ments of the End of Empire Project (BDEEP), produced primarily in the 1990s and published by the Stationery Office, provide some of the official somewhat sanitized story given the protracted process of approving files for public release. Meanwhile, the oral histories of the Overseas Service Pensioners' Association (OSPA), generated mainly in the first half of the first decade of the twenty-first century, offer insights into the real, unofficial, idiosyncratic processes. In turn, these are augmented by the oral history project at the Commonwealth and Empire Museum in Bristol. And all such published (auto)biographies and memoirs have been tabulated in Terry Barringer's exhaustive annotated bibliography, now going into its expanded second edition.[11] These constitute interesting segues into the initial period of international development: from Marshall to Colombo Plans. In short, in part because of post-war preoccupations with the Cold War, the Commonwealths constituted something of a sideshow to the global sagas of bipolarity and decolonization, although they in fact advanced and moderated both.

Such histories or inheritances inform today's Commonwealths. The networks they generated advance contemporary informal nexuses like the largely intergovernmental Commonwealth Organizations Group (COG) and nongovernmental Civil Society Advisory Committee (CSAC) to the Foundation. Similarly, interests and issues get advanced through such idiosyncrasies as the annual Commonwealth Day and Commonwealth Lecture. More formal, less intimate, international organizations like the UN lack such flexible mechanisms for identifying or addressing problems and getting pressing issues into the public domain. So, for instance, the inter-faith Commonwealth Day service in Westminster Abbey, animated by the Council of Commonwealth Societies in London, provides an opportunity for different communities to indicate their pragmatism, especially relevant to the post-7/7 and 9/11 world of multi-cultural and multi-faith communities. While the Commonwealth Lecture provides platforms for leading figures in the Commonwealth to advance original perspectives, such as the Bangladeshi 2006 Nobel Prize Laureate Mohammad Yunus on microcredit for development in 2003 and James Wolfensohn in 2006 suggesting that there is another emerging post-bipolar "three worlds" of global development (see Chapter 5).

I describe the evolution and organization of some of the formal structures and processes of the Commonwealths in later chapters, but here mention a couple of less formal and less familiar dimensions, which might constitute the more salient reasons for the Commonwealths' surprising longevity and resilience despite minimal resources and multiple detractors. Increasingly, global issues get discovered, defined and advanced by non-state think tanks and semi-state coalitions. Other international agencies have their own think tanks such as Human Development Research Office (HDRO (UNDP)), UN Research Institute for Social Development (UNRISD) and UN University (UNU), World Bank Institute (WBI) and OECD Development Centre. By contrast, the Commonwealth can seek input and support from the very modest and rather fragile Commonwealth Policy Studies Unit and Institute for Commonwealth Studies at the University of London *inter alia*.

Here I suggest further analysis of Commonwealth Organizations' Group (COG) and Civil Society Advisory Committee (CSAC) (to the Foundation) (see Chapter 2) as sources of ideas, policies and cohesion for the network. The latter global group assembles but once a year, appointed by the Foundation to reflect if not represent leading organizations and directions from civil societies and NGOs in the several regions of the Commonwealths. However, every other year it assembles twice as it also helps animate CPF as in Malta in late 2005 and Kampala in late 2007. It is more institutionalized and recognized than the former, which operates as something of an informal London-based "kitchen cabinet" meeting several times per annum, along the lines of, say, the Academic Council for the UN System (ACUNS) for the UN or Global Development Network (GDN) for the IBRD.

Moreover, one can identify something of an informal division of labor between Secretariat and Foundation, sometimes involving "subcontracting" from the former to the latter to minimize "political" tensions? Likewise, both sides of Marlborough House can pass apparently difficult matters on to appropriate professional associations or civil society associates for an initial airing.

Together, such somewhat idiosyncratic informal arrangements often advanced through personal connections and networks, along with the range of Commonwealth Plus organizations, constitute a distinctive Commonwealth "public diplomacy": a changeable range of inter- and non-state agencies addressing a continuously evolving set of global issues, thereby advancing Commonwealth governance: intergovernmental as well as non-official but not overly proud of their prerogatives.

Redefining multilateralisms and public diplomacy

The Commonwealths have displayed a capacity since World War II to assist in overcoming or at least transcending or containing international issues. I would point to two in particular since 1945 as an indication of potential roles in the unexpectedly difficult world of the new millennium. I return to these in the next, historical chapter.

First, the very transition from a "British" Commonwealth of white Dominions, owing "common allegiance to the Crown" as imperial head, to a multiracial association of independent states, including republics, would not have occurred in the late 1940s without a degree of pragmatism on both sides, especially on the side of India. The willingness to negotiate and accept the London Declaration in 1949 was a turning point. India, along with (West and East) Pakistan, became member republics in 1950 although Ireland did withdraw then, never to return.

But when Bangladesh (East Pakistan) achieved independence from (West) Pakistan in 1975 it was accepted as a new member.

And second, when both Secretariat and Foundation were brand-new organizations in the mid-1960s, the Commonwealths were confronted by Ian Smith's racist Unilateral Declaration of Independence (UDI) in Rhodesia. As elaborated in the next chapter, they both spent the next quarter-century focused on achieving majority democratic rule in Southern Africa. The return of South Africa as a member in mid-1994 after more than three decades—it had left on becoming a republic in mid-1961—marked the end of this historic anti-apartheid period, although the unhappy saga of Zimbabwe's suspension then withdrawal at the turn of the century is symptomatic of the incompleteness of some such transitions.

The Commonwealths may, then, yet have an opportunity to play again on the global stage as they first did post-World War II and again as an authoritative "epistemic" community seeking to overcome racist regimes in Southern Africa in the 1970s and 1980s[12] as indicated in Chapter 3 onwards. And such a possibility is in part a function of them having not played a role to date in traditional national or global security arenas.

Human security along with human development and human rights is unlikely to be realized through a "war" on terrorism in the first decade of the new century, just as the wars on poverty and on drugs have not been won. Rather, the very multi-cultural, multi-racial and multi-faith character of the Commonwealths and their members may yet lead toward novel forms of communication and "confidence-building" among disparate communities who at least share some histories and values. As indicated further in Chapters 5 and 6, post-CHOGM in Malta, both Secretariat and Foundation are considering ways to advance interaction and cooperation amongst different communities in the worldwide Commonwealths.

Such possible contemporary roles reflect the potential for new multilateralisms and public diplomacy around the Commonwealths which help distinguish it from other global institutions analyzed in this Routledge series. As Peter Vale and David Black suggested as South Africa qualified to rejoin the network:

> The Commonwealth has many personalities: international organization, global network, diplomatic club, amongst others. Underpinning these, however, is an intricate and complex set of linkages, from the ACU to the CPA. These professional associations are, in many ways, the glue which holds the Commonwealth together.[13]

The initial impetus for the official "British" Commonwealth was inter-(white) Dominion relations facilitated through "High Commissions" even if not all the founding countries, given their considerable indigenous communities, were really white. It then became the midwife for decolonization, especially in Africa but also in the islands of the Caribbean and Pacific. And out of the extended trauma of the rebirth of the multiracial communities of Southern Africa came its contemporary focus: good governance for human development, human rights and human security. As McIntyre asserts, reflecting on the 1991 Harare Principles, etc.: "The old club had become a rules-based international association."[14]

Although in the most recent full-length enquiry into the official ComSec, Krishnan Srinivasan laments the disinterest of the British government in the Commonwealth,[15] others claim that ownership by the other 52 member states is preferable in terms of continuing contributions to development, governance, multilateralism, and so forth. By contrast to Srinivasan's lamentations, Ford and Katwala insist that "It is time to destroy the myth of the 'British Commonwealth'"[16] (see more in Chapter 6 below).

Nevertheless, despite any pretensions arising from the illusions of empire, the Commonwealth was never more than a minority of the world's states or peoples or economies. Until the late 1960s—the decolonization decade in Africa—the inter-state Commonwealth was but 10 to 15 percent of the size of the UN. By the 1970s it was 25 percent. And, as the 1980s turned into the 1990s, it had some 50 members compared to the UN's 150, i.e. some 33 percent. But now that there are some 200 states, the Commonwealth's proportion has declined again to just over a quarter (see Appendix 1). Yet its members include OECD and NICs, emerging economies as well as LLDCs and fragile states (see Tables I.1 and I.2). And if it comes to include OTs as, say, associate members in future then its percentage of global state actors would increase once again.

Meanwhile, its impact on other non-anglophone Commonwealths has been considerable: they largely exist in response to the anglophone network, something of a backhanded compliment to the impact of the intergovernmental grouping and its nongovernmental associates?

Other non-anglophone post-imperial Commonwealths

The post-imperial anglophone ComSec and related elements in the formal and informal Commonwealths stand in contrast to the post-colonial intergovernmental associations arising from the legacies of other empires. Here I identify six other groupings, the first three or four of which are clearly post-colonial parallels. The final pair—Nordic and Islamic states—are more *sui generis*, though they share some common features in their emphasis on language and culture or religion. These half-dozen groupings are unlikely to appear in any of the other titles in the present Global Institutions series as they have even less visibility or recognition than the anglophone Commonwealths.

Although not as numerous in national memberships as *la francophonie*, the Commonwealths are more comprehensive in their activities— e.g. corporate and cultural, educational and peoples' Commonwealths—and aura as well as more numerous in terms of population. Indeed, they tend to set the pace for the others, with other ex-imperial networks tending to follow and emulate as indicated in the timing of their institutionalization and innovations.

Even Srinivasan comments positively on the impact of British colonialism and Commonwealth on other non-anglophone communities in terms of emulation and competition:

> The Commonwealth was the inspiration for the French Union and the Community, and later, the *Organisation de la francophonie*. It was one of the models for the Dutch-Indonesian Union, and the prototype of the Community of Portuguese-speaking countries. It served as a bridge between the Empire and the post-colonial period.[17]

I treat the half-dozen parallels below, the Danish and Dutch "commonwealths" having become rather modest, essentially bi- rather than multilateral financial and educational links amongst two small sets of non-metropolitan communities (e.g. Faroes and Greenland and the Antilles and Surinam, respectively).

First, *la francophonie* now consists of some 55 states and a dozen Associates or Observers, not all of which are actually French-speaking societies, mainly in Africa and Europe but also Canada (the provinces of Quebec and New Brunswick also participate), the Caribbean and Southeast Asia. Associate members include Bulgaria, Cape Verde, Egypt, Equatorial Guinea, Guinea-Bissau, Rumania, Sao Tome and Principe, and St. Lucia, some of which have virtually no francophone citizens. *La francophonie* was always less affluent and more African than the Commonwealth, so France tried to get it to emulate and better the anglophone Commonwealth.

The first summit of the francophone community was, symbolically, at Versailles in 1986 and it has since held meetings in Cotonou, Mauritius, Vietnam, etc., but mainly in French and Canadian (e.g. Moncton 1999) cities; the most recent, the eleventh, was in Bucharest in late 2006. It has evolved from *Agence de Cooperation Culturelle et Technique* (ACCT) in 1970 through *Agence Intergouvernementale de la Francophonie* (AIF) to *Organisation Internationale de la Francophonie* (OIF) in 1998. It includes some dimensions of the anglophone Commonwealths like games and universities but not others like CBC or CHRI. Despite the dilution of the grouping by the admittance of non- or only semi-francophone countries, Srinivasan suggests that "*La francophonie* is one of the few international organizations where cultural goals are held as paramount."[18] Nine Commonwealth states (eleven if the two Canadian provinces are included) are also members (or Associate members or Observers) of *la francophonie*.

Second, seven lusophone states formed the *Comunidade dos Paises de Lingua Portuguesa* (CPLP) (Community of Portuguese Language Countries) in 1996, dominated by Brazil and Portugal, in reaction to Mozambique joining the Commonwealth in 1995. East Timor is its most recent, eighth, member joining on independence from Indonesia in 2002, but the remaining five are African. Srinivasan comments that "In contrast to the Commonwealth, the CPLP was a long time in the conception—a full 23 years after Portugal's escape from the authoritarian rule that enabled the colonies to achieve their independence."[19] He had noted earlier in his book that, unlike the anglophone Commonwealth, "The CPLP was conditioned by, but was not a product of decolonization since it came on the scene long after the decolonization process had been completed."[20]

Third, the 21 Spanish-speaking or Hispanic states also waited until the 1990s to create the *Organizacion de Estados Iberoamericanos* (Organization of Ibero-American States (OEI)), including Puerto Rico and Equatorial Guinea as well as Argentina and Mexico. Srinivasan notes that compared to the CPLP,

> The OEI had an even more languorous start. . . . It evolved slowly into . . . an organization under the leadership of heads of state and government in 1991. It now meets at the summit annually, with a predominant position held by Spain and Portugal, who use the Organization to raise their profile in Europe while defending the interests of the Latin American members in the EU.[21]

Fourth, following the end of the Cold War, 11 ex-Russian states (Turkmenistan became an associate rather than full member in mid-2005) founded the post-Soviet Commonwealth of Independent States (CIS) in 1991. To be sure, the CIS is still dominated by Russia with the half-dozen "stans" also being central, but it also includes old

Soviet allies like Belarus and Ukraine and small Central European states like Georgia and Moldova. By contrast to the above four networks, the final pair of "commonwealths" are based on inheritances or identities around language or religion rather than recent history or empire.

Fifth, a religious- rather than language-based grouping is the Organization of the Islamic Conference (OIC), with headquarters in Jeddah, Saudi Arabia, 11 of the 57 members of which are in the Commonwealth. Its affiliated agencies include private companies and civil societies including the Islamic Development Bank.

And finally, a grouping which is neither language- nor religion-centered: five Nordic states and three autonomous territories connected through parliaments and mutual interests, and shared history and ecology, including links with the ex-Soviet bloc, including the CIS. The Nordic community is like the anglophone Commonwealths in that democratic values are central. But the Nordic community is different from the other commonwealths as it lacks a single global language (other than English), though most except Finnish are mutually intelligible. And the Nords have no immediate imperial power, although the Swedes have a long history of dominance and the Russian empire was a post-war threat and catalyst. However, the degree to which the Nordic states are similar and the degree to which they are still social democratic or neutral is increasingly problematic, although they are all democratic polities and capitalist economies. They have very different, often complicated, relations with the EU, for example.

In conclusion to this section, I turn in Chapter 6 to a somewhat bizarre and certainly very conservative reformulation or revival of the original anglophone world, including the United States, the first rebel British colony. As we will see, there some US conservatives have begun to advocate an "anglosphere" to advocate an English-speaking "civilization" in which certain selective traditional values are advanced.

Despite their characteristic British-style self-effacement, the anglophone Commonwealths are widely recognized to be different from, possibly superior to, their counterparts in other post-imperial language communities. Indeed, as already noted, the others exist largely in reaction to the anglophone network. By contrast to such emulation at the global level, the potential inter-regional role of the Commonwealths is treated next.

Commonwealths and new regionalisms

The Commonwealths' membership is concentrated in five regions of the world, mainly in the South; it lacks governmental representation in, say, Central Europe or Central Asia or the Middle East although, as indicated in the next chapter, some of the small Gulf states could claim an inheritance of "informal" association with the British empire. Members are presently located in Africa (18 states), the Americas (13), Pacific (11), Asia (8) and Europe (3). Given such concentrations, Commonwealth states constitute important and influential caucuses in a specific, finite set of regional organizations. As McIntyre notes:

> With the transformation of the Commonwealth following the acceleration of decolonization after 1960, and the simultaneous decline of Britain as a power, regionalism burgeoned.[22]

Commonwealth connections are salient amongst some but not all regional groupings, especially not amongst the other post-imperial communities above (e.g. not CPLP, OEI, OIC or the post-Soviet CIS or newer Shanghai Cooperation Organization) other than *la francophonie* (* indicates that Commonwealth members constitute more than half the total):

* Association of Southeast Asian Nations (ASEAN) (3/10 members)
* African Union (AU) and NEPAD (18/53)
* Caribbean Community (CARICOM) (11/12)*
* Colombo Plan (11/25)
* Common Market for Eastern and Southern Africa (COMESA) (9/20)
* East African Community (EAC) (3/3)*
* Economic Community of West African States (ECOWAS) (4/16)
* Indian Ocean Rim Association for Regional Cooperation (IOR-ARC) (10/14)*
* Intergovernmental Authority for Development (IGAD) (2/7)
* Nile Basin Initiative (3/9)
* Pacific Forum (13/16)*
* Southern African Development Community (SADC) (10/14)*
* South Asian Association for Regional Cooperation (SAARC) (5/7)*
* Southern African Customs Union (SACU) (5/5), etc.*

Commonwealth states are also not unimportant members of the G8 (Britain and Canada), EU (Britain, Cyprus and Malta out of 25/27), NAFTA (Canada), OAS (12/35), etc.

Commonwealth participation in such overlapping regional structures can lead to two-way interaction: from the regions to the Commonwealth and vice versa. As indicated in the next chapter, African members used the then-new ComSec to advance majority rule and independence in the settler states of Southern Africa. Relatedly, the

Commonwealth connection was central in the establishment then evolution of SADCC into SADC; indeed, SADCC was largely a donor-driven initiative to advance development and moderation in the increasingly liberated countries of the region. And Commonwealth states constitute the overwhelming majority in the Caribbean, Indian and Pacific ocean networks along with revived and redefined EAC, as indicated above by those regional institutions marked with an asterix; i.e. its regional connections reinforce its global emphases on development, small island states, trade, and so on.

In short, given such roles, I would argue that the Commonwealths can be considered to have begun to contribute analytic insights into the definition and contribution of the embryonic conceptualization of "new regionalisms"—i.e. less economistic or state-centric—by contrast to established or traditional regional integration studies or cases like the EU, etc. In so doing, they advance the contrasts pursued by UNU-CRIS in its own concentration on comparisons between "old" EU, now of the 25/27, and "new" African regionalisms, both aspects of the burgeoning analysis and practice of global governance.

Commonwealths and global governance in the twenty-first century

The conceptualization and realization of global governance were amongst the positive aspirations of the end of bipolarity in the 1990s. But the salience and sustainability of such governance are increasingly problematic because of the over-reaction in the new century to fundamentalist terrorism by some of the leading national security states like the United States and UK. Their "wars" on terrorism make notions like global governance more controversial as well as problematic. Hence the imperative of less central or visible global institutions like the Commonwealths in keeping such ideas alive through the development of alternative concepts like Commonwealth governance.

Like many contemporary concepts, including Weiss' opening citation to this chapter, that of global governance emerged from or was advanced by an international organization or think tank rather than the academy: i.e. from a UN Commission with the same name. It proposed a rather generic, pragmatic definition of the term:

> Governance is the sum of the many ways individuals and institutions, public and private, manage their common affairs. It is a continuing process through which conflicting or diverse interests may be accommodated and cooperative action may be taken. It

includes formal institutions and regimes empowered to enforce compliance, as well as informal arrangements that people and institutions either have agreed to or perceive to be in their interest. ...

At the global level, governance has been viewed primarily as intergovernmental relationships, but it must now be understood as also involving NGOs, citizens' movements, multinational corporations and the global capital market. Interacting with these are global mass media.[23]

The Commission's formulation and description, partially in response to the pressures and possibilities of globalization, are compatible with evolving Commonwealth practice. Its report sought "to demonstrate how changes in the global situation have made improved arrangements for the governance of international affairs imperative."[24] Unhappily, this is ever more so today than a decade ago.

As already suggested, the Commonwealths of more than 50 states and more than 70 professional associations spanning South and North are able to advance a range of new multilateralisms to identify and address a range of new global issues, from continuing concerns like education, gender and health to current issues like migrations of professionals in sectors like education and health, money-laundering in island jurisdictions, etc. They do so by incorporating all three "sides" of the governance triangle into their programming; i.e. as already indicated, the two bottom non-state corners of civil society and the private sector as well as the point of the triangle: the state.

Enlightened perspectives are even more needed in the twenty-first century than at the end of the twentieth. The latter was characterized by an over-optimism approaching naivety about an imminent peace dividend and about the benefits of political and economic liberalizations. Despite the ongoing rhetoric about democracy, profound threats to it are arising from growing fears of fundamentalisms and terrorisms. So the Commonwealths' continuing concern about interrelated human development, human rights and human security is now more needed yet more endangered than ever. Its non- as well as interstate networks are becoming essential to the protection of gains against the claims of national security or homeland defense let alone to further advance the frontiers of democracy.

Commonwealth networks, which span the inter- and nongovernmental divide, mirror the generic definition of "advocacy networks" advanced by Keck and Sikkink:

Major actors in advocacy networks may include the following: 1) international and domestic nongovernmental research and advocacy organizations; 2) local social movements; 3) foundations; 4) the media; 5) churches, trade unions, consumer organizations and intellectuals; 6) parts of regional and international intergovernmental organizations; and 7) parts of the executive and/or parliamentary branches of governments. Not all of these will be present in each advocacy network ... NGOs introduce new ideas, provide information and lobby for policy changes.[25]

In the Commonwealths and elsewhere, the balance amongst these heterogeneous institutions or networks will vary between foci and over time, with the trend toward more authoritative roles for non-state actors, both civil society and corporate. But state security apparatuses have had a new lease of life since 9/11, especially since 7/7 and the recognition of home-grown terrorism in London. Over-reactions by intelligence and police organizations threaten to undermine multiracial and multi-faith understanding and tolerance, with profound implications for diverse communities around the Commonwealths. Hence the latter's determination to begin to confront such issues, however uncomfortable, and despite its lack of either familiarity or resources in this delicate area as outlined in Chapter 5 below.

Parallel to both globalization and liberalization, the Commonwealths have witnessed an expansion in the scale and scope of civil society activity: from the relatively familiar terrain of education and health and even gender to ecology, indigenous communities, rights, security, etc. These have served to define and reinforce the embryonic notion of Commonwealth governance (see Appendix 3).

Facilitated by the Foundation, non-state actors have certainly come to play a greater role in the Commonwealths over the last decade than ever before, reflective of their expanding global leverage. But such creativity does not always endear them to some member regimes, especially those that remain outside the ranks of the Foundation's supporters. And some current global issues inevitably pit non-state actors against inter-state institutions as I note in Chapter 4 below.

As Schreuder suggests in an opening citation above, the day of the Commonwealths may, then, finally have come: not as leading global institutions but rather as more informal, flexible, nexuses which can respond more readily and pragmatically to emerging global issues like alienation within diasporas and continuing global migrations of professional communities. As Mills and Stremlau note, the Commonwealth

happens to comply with "current requirements for international organizations: being flexible and decentralized, cost-effective and cooperative,
and not suffering from potentially paralyzing structural weak-
nesses."[26] I turn in conclusion to the impacts of new technologies on
the roles and impacts of the Commonwealths as reflected in the range
of websites at the end of the book.

Commonwealth networks and the Internet

The expanded flow of communications around a growing number of
issues amongst an increasing number of heterogeneous actors which
characterizes Commonwealth governance requires novel technology,
as now offered by the Internet. Global advocacy around the Ottawa
and Kimberley Processes, for example, could hardly have been envi-
saged let along sustained without email: how else to manage the 1,400
actors in the International Campaign to Ban Landmines (ICBL)?
Likewise, global communications from Internet to couriers, airfreight
to containers, mean that there is no longer any particular reason for
Commonwealth agencies to be concentrated in London. CHRI has
always been in Delhi, and now has branches in Accra and London.
COL is in Vancouver and CAPAM in Toronto. The CJA has been in
Trinidad and is moving on to Toronto. And the CPU is considering
relocating to India, possibly to that icon of globalization, Bangalore
(now officially Bengalooru).

The post-bipolar era was characterized by not only the expansion of
"global civil society" but also the rapid development of global information technology (IT). The coincidence of exponential economic and
political liberalization with the parallel worldwide reach of the Internet in the 1990s facilitated transnational networking as a feature of
the "globalization syndrome." Because English is the *lingua franca* of
the global economy as well as of the dominant national economy—the
United States—it also became the primary language of the Internet.
In turn, this has served to facilitate communication within the anglophone Commonwealths. I turn to the Commonwealths as a "network
of networks" in the concluding chapters.

Cable and Wireless (CandW) was the early company and technology which constituted "the thin red line" of telecommunications which
kept the empire in touch, as sail and steam ships had done initially. It
laid the initial underwater fiber system between London and Australia,
Canada, the Caribbean, the Mediterranean, Hong Kong, India, etc. in
the late nineteenth and early twentieth centuries. But with the subsequent combination of liberalization, privatizations and technological

change like mobile phones and the Internet (as suggested by my penultimate concluding paragraph to this book, Blackberries are imperative for today's senior ComSec bureaucrats), CandW's fixed-line role has diminished to serving a few independent islands and OTs although it still provides corporate communications globally.

The Commonwealth Telecommunications Organization (CTO) has likewise evolved along with the telecoms industry from imperial institution of state enterprises to post-colonial network of private providers. It celebrated its centenary in 2001, having become an independent international organization in 1967. In addition to 33 Commonwealth state members it now has another 15–20 independent and dependent territories as Associate members. Its range of activities embraces non-Commonwealth ICT corporations and associations, especially now extending to the burgeoning world of mobile and digital telecommunications. Its programming includes annual forums (Yaounde, Cameroon 2005; London 2006), myriad projects, scholarships, etc. The CTO has also been active around issues of MDGs, digital divide and domain governance, as identified further below, bringing North and South together without being diverted by the unilateralism of the United States.

In turn, Commonwealth governance has become more extensive and accessible because of the contemporary global development of IT architecture. Thus, for a relatively modest investment, the work of Commonwealth professional agencies in democracy (e.g. CPA), education (e.g. ACU and COL), ecology, gender, human rights (e.g. CHRI and CJA) and literature (the Commonwealth Writers' Prize is celebrating two decades in 2007) has been made readily available throughout the Commonwealth and the rest of the world. The Internet also permits anyone to track the activities of global institutions like the UN and IFIs, arguably increasing their accountability and transparency. And it has enabled the Commonwealths to reduce the negative consequences and high costs of widely disbursed communities which include islands in the Caribbean, Indian Ocean, Mediterranean and South Pacific. Symptomatic of the ability of Commonwealth Plus to mitigate the negative consequences of distance and size at the start of the twenty-first century is the proposal and process for a Virtual University for Small States of the Commonwealth being advanced by COL.

To be sure, as recognized in CHOGM Communiqués, the "digital divide" has somewhat retarded and complicated Commonwealth governance as less affluent countries and communities have been less able to keep up with changing global standards for the World Wide Web. However, while the South may have had difficulty in expanding band width for the Internet, it has also been able to leap-frog technologies for the telephone by the rapid widespread adoption of wireless mobiles or cells around the turn of the century.

Moreover, because of the combination of distance and language, many of the contemporary developments in IT have come from Commonwealth member states; not just large (at least in territory) developed economies like Canada but also large (in population and territory) less developed economies with advanced sectors like India. Thus the former is the home of IT icons like the Blackberry from RIM (now a central feature of Commonwealth diplomacy, as recognized in the final chapter) while the latter is the base of a remarkable set of IT innovators like Infosys, NIIT, Reliance, Tata and Wipro. The latter are a reflection of the advantages of English-language higher education and related institutions along with professional migrations and diasporas in the anglophone world of high-tech concentrated in places such as Silicon Valley in California. It is not a coincidence that centers of IT innovation are found in the Commonwealth, such as Waterloo in Canada, and the Indian Silicon Plateau: the technology triangle of Bangalore (now Bengalooru), Chennai and Hyderabad in India (see Chapter 4 below).

Advancing the Valetta summit's focus on networking for development, in mid-2006 a trio of developing, emerging Commonwealth economies joined Malta as CHOGM host in creating an ICT development program to help transcend any remaining digital divide: "Commonwealth Connects." India, Mozambique and Trinidad along with Malta (i.e. mainly "developmental states") have contributed 1 million pounds sterling to facilitate links over a three-year period. Its first program is to look at how ICTs facilitate change after a disaster, using the case of the Christmas 2004 tsunami, which served to reinvigorate SIDS as an established concentration of the Commonwealths.

After this somewhat conceptual overview, I turn in the next chapter back to the early, unpropitious origins of the Commonwealths; but I return to issues around the Commonwealths and globalization, including global as well as Commonwealth studies, in Chapter 4. Between the wars the British Commonwealth was rooted in more rather than less intergovernmental arrangements, initially largely amongst the white Dominions but always with the Indian Raj being a major feature and focus. Although the numbers of member states grew significantly after World War II, and notwithstanding the well established status of the first generation of professional institutions (e.g. ACU, CPA, CPU then CGF), the place of non-state institutions remained rather ambiguous and uncertain until the end of the Cold War. Then, together, liberalization and globalization served to enhance the roles of both civil society and the private sector. I turn to such contemporary issues and possibilities in the second half of the book, after surveying the Commonwealths' earlier post-colonial histories in Chapter 2.

2   From decolonization to democratization

Beyond the original extended family to post-imperial nation-building?

> In the broad historical perspective, the Commonwealth changed during the middle third of the century, from being a small, white, imperial club to a large multilateral, international association. The Balfour Declaration of 1926 proclaimed the doctrine of equality. The London Declaration of 1949 facilitated republican membership, confirmed multiracialism and created the symbolic Headship. The Singapore Declaration of 1971 made equality and multiracialism dynamic principles to be pursued in international affairs.
>
> (David McIntyre)[1]

The Commonwealths are one of the unintended consequences of unplanned decolonization, even although the left in the British Labour Party had long advocated national independence and international organization. As indicated in the concluding chapter, the inter- and non-state Commonwealths emerged out of inter-war long-range planning and post-war short-term imperatives around demobilization, decolonization and democratization. In the first decade of the twentieth century, the Dominions had agreed to "Imperial Conferences" among those colonies with "responsible government": Australia, Britain, Canada, Newfoundland, New Zealand and South Africa, plus India from 1917 and Ireland from 1922. And from 1954, their concerns and deliberations happened to be largely compatible with other major dimensions of post-war multilateralism, namely the UN and IFI systems. Although several of the victorious allies were "old" Commonwealth—i.e. Australia, Canada, India, New Zealand, South Africa and the UK—the primary regional foci of post-war planning were Western Europe and East Asia rather than, say, Sub-Saharan Africa or South Asia. And it soon became apparent that the British empire was in no financial state to resist myriad nationalist pressures arising in most of its imperial outposts, themselves encouraged by invaluable wartime service by hundreds of thousands of soldiers from the colonies with the Allies in Europe and Asia.

However, early decolonization in South Asia was easier than late decolonization in Southern Africa. Dismantling the Raj proceeded readily before 1950; overturning settler colonialism in the 1970s and 1980s was considerably more problematic and painful, entailing considerable risks for the newly institutionalized, multi-racial Commonwealths. The post-war recognition of three Dominions or republics in South Asia followed eventually, a quarter-century later around the end of the Cold War, by another trio in Southern Africa, marked turning points for the Commonwealths.

The admission of the new republics of Ceylon, India and Pakistan in the late 1940s enabled the Commonwealths to transcend their white Dominion inheritance. The independence of Zimbabwe, then Namibia and finally South Africa from 1980 onwards permitted them to increasingly insist on good governance as a condition of membership. As apartheid and bipolarity came to an end in the early 1990s, the Commonwealths were better able to begin to advance human development, human rights and human security for at least a quarter of the world's states and a third of its peoples, as indicated in the next chapter. David McIntyre suggests, perhaps somewhat optimistically, that the Commonwealths enjoyed something of a renaissance in the 1990s.[2]

In some ways, the modern Commonwealth was inaugurated by the London Declaration which allowed for republican membership, so ComSec could celebrate the jubilee in 1999 (see the analysis of celebratory reflections and projections in Chapter 6), even although the formal institutionalization of both Secretariat and Foundation was properly marked as just four decades some six years later in 2005. There was a parallel confusion over nomenclature, with the transition from "British Empire" to "British Commonwealth" at the end of the war yielding to the simple "Commonwealth" by the 1970s without adjectival reference to either Britain or empire.[3]

This chapter transits from the different forms and eras of transitions in South Asia and Southern Africa to the contemporary Commonwealths' regular major global events: CHOGM and the Games, every two and four years, respectively. Both these interrelated transitions and events have advanced the Commonwealths' own estimations and dimensions of globalization as larger and wider membership has advanced broader mega-events which are increasingly global in terms of hosting and attendance. I turn to continuing international and inter-city competition to host such global events in Chapter 5 below.

At its height at the turn of the twentieth century, the British empire controlled a quarter of the world's territories and peoples, but it was already in decline: it had risen in the seventeenth century but begun to stagnate in the eighteenth. Aside from its "formal" imperialism of colonies and protectorates, centered on the Indian Raj, the British world included a fluid range of territories within an "informal" empire concentrated in the Middle East. As we will see in the final chapter, the latter set of countries—from the Gulf to Afghanistan, Egypt, Iraq, Iran and Sudan—become important again in current considerations of membership criteria and expressions of interest.

South Asia: republican status

Between the wars, the white Dominions—Australia, Canada, New Zealand and South Africa—demanded and achieved a growing degree of autonomy or independence. McIntyre suggests that "The story of Dominion status ... is unique in the history of decolonization and represents the Commonwealth's contribution to one of the great transitions of the twentieth century."[4] India likewise, as the "jewel in the crown," received increasing recognition if not autonomy. But Ireland remained constitutionally problematic and physically partitioned. Its republican status was more tenuous than that of India, so in the spring of 1949 Ireland exited while India (1949) along with Ceylon (1948) and Pakistan (1947) but without Burma, joined as "Dominions." So, as other global multilateral agencies like the UN and IFI systems were being established, the anglophone empire was also in an intense process of metamorphosis: "The coincidence of two republics moving in opposite directions at the same time is only one of the great ironies of the occasion."[5]

India has always held a unique significance in the Commonwealths, in part because of its scale and diversity as the world's largest democracy as well as its several generations of myriad diasporas throughout the global community, especially the Commonwealths (see Chapter 4 below on this and other such diasporas). But like many "new states" it was diverted for much of its first half century by aspirations of "socialist" planning and development, in its case reinforced during the Cold War by the imperative of a strategic alliance with the Soviet Union given the combination of US support for Pakistan and Chinese antagonism. The end of bipolarity allowed the Indian state and political economy to begin to redefine themselves away from restrictive notions of mixed economy and non-alignment and toward more entrepreneurial, competitive roles. Unlike, say, Singapore, India never achieved recognition as a newly industrializing country (NIC) in the late twentieth century. But at the start of the twenty-first century it is unquestionably one of the four BRICs, increasingly classed as emerging economies, along with Brazil, Russia and China. And, as we will see in Chapters 4 and 5 below, it is the only one of these four that can claim and exploit its anglophone legacy and now democratic inheritance and connections.

Southern Africa: liberation struggles

If the inclusion of South Asia and then much of Sub-Saharan Africa into the Commonwealth was relatively painless, despite Sudan choosing not to join in 1956, decolonization in settler-controlled Southern Africa was problematic and traumatic, pitting the new global South, especially Africa, against the post-imperial center. Following Ghana in 1957, Africa's largest country—Nigeria—became a member of the Commonwealth in 1960, the year of British prime minister Harold Macmillan's "Wind of Change" speech in the (white) South African parliament in Cape Town. Although Commonwealth membership increased fourfold from 1950 to 1970, particularly in the 1960s—the decade of Africa—white minority regimes below the Zambezi remained intransigent. Thus the Rhodesian Front settler regime of Ian Smith declared a Unilateral Declaration of Independence (UDI) in Salisbury soon after the Secretariat was formally established in London in 1965.

Britain was in a minority of one (or two if Menzies' conservative opinions are taken into account as prime minister of Australia) over UDI in the Commonwealth, symbolized by the first CHOGMs to be held outside London: a special meeting in Lagos in early 1966 and a regular summit in Singapore in 1971. Despite endless diplomacy, the conflict inside and around the country escalated, leading eventually to the Lancaster House negotiations in London in late 1979. These led to a new constitution with Commonwealth military and election observer groups, although the absence of a truth and reconciliation process may have contributed to subsequent bitterness, as revealed in the Commonwealth's suspension of the Mugabe regime in March 2002 and Zimbabwe's subsequent departure in late 2003.

The "unholy alliance" of the trio of racist regimes in Southern Africa constituted a determined, "regional" resistance to majority rule. The wars in Rhodesia and Southwest Africa intensified after the Portuguese coup of 1974 which removed the *cordon sanitaire* of the lusophone empire. Pressure on the bastion of white rule—the Republic of South Africa—came to involve a mix of economic and other measures, including cultural boycotts, financial sanctions, liberation movement networks, military isolation and sports (especially cricket and rugby) and other pressures.[6] These included a series of boycotts of the Commonwealth Games in the 1970s and 1980s. So in Edinburgh in 1986, more countries boycotted (32) than participated (26), but such pressure had eased by Auckland in 1990 and Victoria in 1994. Non-state networks centered on London were the core of the global anti-apartheid struggle, which included most African and other Southern governments. And the Commonwealth's second secretary-general, Sonny Ramphal, played an increasingly important role in such multilevel diplomacy, including an innovative Commonwealth Eminent Persons Group (EPG) to visit and report in the late 1980s.

Despite the apparent lack of efficacy of such interrelated pressures, the South African regime began to move toward reconciliation as the Cold War ended, with Nelson Mandela released from imprisonment on Robben Island in 1990 after over a quarter-century of incarceration. The Commonwealth facilitated transition if not transformation by inviting him as a guest to the 1991 CHOGM in Harare, where it drew up its statement of membership principles. And South Africa formally returned to the extended family in 1994 with its first formal CHOGM in Auckland in 1995, at which the Nigerian military regime was suspended. South Africa led the world in creating a Truth and Reconciliation Commission (TRC) compatible with Commonwealth values, with relevance for the mid-decade Amartya Sen Commission on respect and understanding (treated in the two closing chapters).

Despite the reluctance of successive British governments, the Commonwealth was at its most influential—arguably an epistemic community[7]—over the quarter-century struggle to end apartheid in Southern Africa. Values articulated and refined then, now inform its continuing determination to advance good governance for human development, human rights and human security, including the unique capacity and willingness to suspend governments who offend them. And Britain never abandoned the Commonwealths as one of its distinctive legacies, despite threats to do so. As McIntyre notes, "By the mid-1990s, with the incubus of UDI and apartheid resolved, Britain was free to rediscover the Commonwealth without the burden of an imperial hangover."[8] And now, while South Africa is not an emerging economy comparable to India, it can claim to be a "developmental state." While not a BRIC, it is increasingly associated with two (i.e. half of the four BRICs) in that category—Brazil and India—in a trilateral extension of the BRICs: India-Brazil-South Africa (IBSA) as a centerpiece of the new Southern G20.

Commonwealth summits and other mega-events

As the Commonwealth evolved from empire and gradually became institutionalized, the Imperial then Prime Ministers' Conferences metamorphosed to reflect decolonization processes and republican choices into Commonwealth Heads of Government Meetings (CHOGMs). In turn, as national leaders became busier and more Commonwealth business was transacted in other sectoral summits like Education, Health, Finance, Law, Sports, Tourism, Women and Youth, their leisurely reflections at 10 Downing Street and then Marlborough House in London, including weekend retreats at the UK PM's country house—Chequers—became more compressed and less elegant, as indicated in Appendix 2: down to two-to-three day long weekends by century's turn. And, after a transitional period in the late 1960s as ComSec became institutionalized and UDI was the focus of attention, CHOGMs were held anywhere but London (although in 1977 and 1997 they were back in the UK, in London and Edinburgh respectively), having been hosted only in the imperial metropole for the two decades following World War II, from 1944 to 1965.

Until the turn of the century, they could be readily described along the following lines by David McIntyre:

> For all the variety of place and personality, the contemporary CHOGMs have evolved a well-established pattern, which includes five main features: ceremonial and ritual; political responses to world events; the on-going work of the Commonwealth; getting together at various levels; and the communiqués.[9]

The parallel nongovernmental program, including an NGO forum and exhibition, became institutionalized between Edinburgh and Durban in the late 1990s and the third leg—the Business Forum—became a regular feature between Durban and Abuja. The Youth Summit likewise became established around century's turn, between Edinburgh and Durban. As part of the fallout from the terrorist attacks in the US on 9/11, the first CHOGM of the twenty-first century was, symptomatically, postponed from Brisbane in late 2001, taking place early in the following year on the Queensland coast at an isolated resort at Coolum, but without either the energy or synergy of the parallel Commonwealth People's Forum (CPF). In short, Edinburgh in 1997 featured the first Business, Peoples and Youth Forums, coinciding with Britain's "Year of the Commonwealth," which went somewhat sour given local difficulties in Scotland and global difficulties elsewhere.

The CHOGM and CPF along with Business and Youth events have become mini global events like the G8 or EU summits. Each one has a distinct logo which mixes generic Commonwealth and local themes and idioms, as in Malta and Uganda. And each involves a major media center and coverage throughout the membership, which is usually the stronger the smaller the state. And while each CHOGM has a theme—Networking for Development in Malta in 2005 and Transforming Commonwealth Societies in Kampala in 2007—these typically get hijacked by some current crisis, such as Zimbabwe's exit at Abuja. The postponement in Australia from 2001 to 2002 was the most serious and symbolic such reality test, symptomatic of the end of the post-bipolar period, an elusive "new world order" which never actually generated much of a "peace dividend" for anyone.

Biennial CHOGMs and related events are all the end products of months of preparatory diplomacy largely around ComSec and the Foundation in Marlborough House, parallel to the roles "sherpas" play in getting the G8 to its annual summit, culminating in the work of the Committee of the Whole (COW). They may also be preceded by the deliberations and conclusions of Expert Groups or High Level Review Groups, the most recent of both being considered at Abuja in 2003, on democracy and development and on the structure of ComSec, respectively. As indicated further in Chapter 5 below, in late November 2007 in Kampala, heads of state will consider the report of the latest Commission, on respect and understanding, chaired by Amartya Sen.

The latest CHOGMs—in Abuja, Nigeria (late 2003) and Valetta, Malta (late 2005)—have been three-day events at most. And the latter involved a welcome and continuing innovation to try to bring CHOGM and CPF together, of relevance to other inter-state institutions like the UN and IFIs: a formal session between foreign ministers and civil society, orchestrated by the new Civil Society Advisory Committee (CSAC) to the Foundation outlined below.

To facilitate collaboration between the two sides of Marlborough House—the official and the unofficial, especially around the biennial CHOGM and CPF—an NGO Liaison Officer was appointed in 1993. The latest appointee is David Kalete (Uganda) from Civicus in South Africa. This joint post has become more central in the new century and has both symbolized and facilitated the expansion of the Foundation's purview from professional associations toward civil society and issues of faith and peace as well as democracy and governance.

In turn, the Foundation has moved beyond occasional consultations with civil society to institutionalize a Civil Society Advisory Committee (CSAC), starting in 1999 before Abuja in 2003. In 2005 at Valetta it helped to organize and animate the CPF. And in the run-up to the CHOGM and CPF in Kampala in late 2007, it facilitated a set of pre-summit events throughout Uganda on central issues: development, ecology, science and technology and security. It is a representative group of 12–15 eminent civil society leaders from Foundation members in the several regions of the Commonwealth such as John Foster (Canada), Joan Grant-Cummings (Caribbean), Rae Julian (New Zealand), Warren Nyamugasira (Uganda), Nelcia Robinson (Caribbean), Rajesh Tandon (India) and Nkoyo Toyo (Nigeria). The first such Advisory Committee played less central a role and was smaller (10 members) yet it likewise included some eminent INGO leaders like Maja Daruwala from India, Ezra Mbogori from Kenya and Zimbabwe, and Kumi Naidoo from South Africa. Symptomatic of the growing recognition of the salience, even centrality, of civil society in the Commonwealths' activities, the theme for CHOGM in Uganda in late 2007 as announced on its website is "Transforming Commonwealth Societies to Achieve Political, Economic and Human Development."

Final Communiqués from CHOGMs are crafted months in advance by the ComSec equivalents of the sherpas who manage each G8 summit. They may be tweaked during the leaders' retreats, but tend to follow a familiar format with some current additions. They may be matched by particular Declarations reflective of hosts' interests and/or topical preoccupations. Thus the 1991 Harare Declaration responded to the Commonwealth's anti-apartheid struggle in Southern Africa as the bastion of South Africa approached majority rule, along with the simultaneous escapes from Soviet rule elsewhere, calling for a set of Commonwealth values which should be effected by members' suspensions if necessary. The fin-de-siècle Fancourt Declaration from South Africa focused on making governance and globalization—political and economic liberalizations—compatible with development. In 2005 the Valetta Communiqué on "Networking the Commonwealth for Development" was balanced by the "Gozo Statement on Vulnerable Small States," reflective of Malta's long-standing preoccupation with and advocacy over island and ocean issues.

The late November 2005 Communiqué from the Malta summit is contained in Appendix 4 and covers the gamut of contemporary global issues with a distinctive Commonwealth slant. Such Commonwealth Communiqués on the state of the world typically overlook major inter-state strategic questions such as today's conflicts in the Middle East and Central Asia. (NB I have bunched some of these into overlapping issues although no topic has changed place by more than one or two paragraphs.):

- Fundamental Political Values and CMAG on the Harare Declaration
- Belize, Cyprus, Guyana
- Tolerance and Respect/Peace and Security/Terrorism
- UN Reform/R2P/ICC/Small Arms and Light Weapons/Arms Trade/Drug Trafficking and Transnational Crime/Landmines
- Human Rights
- Public Financial Management Reform/Combating Corruption/ Recovery and Repatriation of Assets of Illicit Origin
- Migration and Development/Human Trafficking
- Digital Divide
- Commonwealth Fund for Technical Cooperation (CFTC)
- World Economic Situation/Multilateral Trade Issues/Debt Relief/ Investment/Strengthening Financial Systems
- MDGs/NEPAD/Sustainable Development
- Small States/Natural Disasters and Humanitarian Assistance
- Health and HIV/AIDS
- Education/Commonwealth of Learning (COL)
- Gender/Youth/Sport
- Commonwealth Functional Cooperation
- Civil Society/Commonwealth Foundation
- Commonwealth Business Council/Commonwealth Partnership for Technological Management
- Commonwealth Membership.

As the Commonwealths progressed from decolonization to democratization, so definitions of and debates about the latter evolved around CMAG from straightforward notions of civilian versus military rule to more nuanced—and problematic—conceptualizations of fundamental political values, and balances of power between branches of government, and onto tripartite partnerships between states, civil societies and private companies. And contradictorily, while the Commonwealths' real budgets and bureaucracies declined, their agendas expanded to reflect the growing range of global issues, including opposition to extremism and intolerance and support for peace and security, as addressed in the next chapter.

3 Commonwealths today
Toward human development, human rights and human security?

The pair of "peak" institutions in the Commonwealths—Secretariat and Foundation—celebrated four decades in 2005. Yet they remain very modest in terms of budgets and staff even though their reach and reputation may be less so. Without the energies and synergies of the unofficial Commonwealth—from businesses to games and literatures to universities—the extended family would be considerably impoverished. Just as some agencies in the UN system are bigger and better funded than headquarters in New York, so, for example, both CGF and CPA have more members than ComSec (see Maps I.1 and I.2). And one or two others became sufficiently extensive and distinctive that they have formally left the family (e.g. CABI below) or graduated (e.g. CTO) even although they continue to have special relationships with the Commonwealths.

This chapter turns from the two or three official intergovernmental institutions to the myriad unofficial networks that constitute the large proportion of the Commonwealths' interactions, concentrated in familiar Commonwealth sectors like communication, development, education, gender, governance, health and public policy (see Appendix 3). Together they articulate and advocate a largely compatible set of norms and ambitions around human development and human rights and increasingly human security, even if the emphasis and sequence may vary between branches of the extended family as well as over time.

Secretariat

When Britain yielded responsibility for the inter-state Commonwealth to the new Secretariat in the mid-1960s, it had some 40 staff and a budget of less than £200,000. Britain assumed 30 percent of these costs, Canada 29 percent, India 11 percent and Australia 10 percent,

New Zealand and Pakistan contributed 2.4 percent each and all the other 21 members 1.5 percent each. The first secretary-general, Arnold Smith, was from one of the founding Dominions, Canada. He brought several Commonwealth functional agencies—e.g. for agriculture, economics, education, forests, science and telecommunications—into the Secretariat so that by the late 1960s it totaled over 150 and at the end of its first decade almost 300 staff (for thumbnail sketches of the four secretaries-general to the end of 2007 see Box 3.1).

Box 3.1   The four Commonwealth secretaries-general, 1965–2007

Arnold Smith (Canada) (1965–75) had been a senior Canadian diplomat, serving as ambassador to Egypt then the Soviet Union, before becoming the first ever secretary-general of the Commonwealth Secretariat. He had been a Rhodes Scholar at Oxford and after London became Lester B. Pearson Professor of International Affairs in the School of International Affairs at Carleton University in Ottawa until retirement in 1980. Arnold Smith was also sometime chair of the North-South Institute in Ottawa and of the International Peace Academy in New York. His autobiography *Stitches in Time: the Commonwealth and world politics* was published by Beaufort Books in 1963. He died in February 1994.

"Sonny" Ramphal (Guyana) (1975–90) was born in 1928 and after studying law at King's College London rose back in Guyana over two decades to become foreign minister and attorney general in 1972 and minister of justice in 1973. During three terms as secretary-general, the longest tenure to date, he was an advocate for the South especially in the anti-apartheid movement and also served on a series of global commissions: the Brandt Commission on North-South, the Palme Commission on Disarmament and Security, the Brundtland Commission on Environment and Development, the Independent Commission on International Humanitarian Issues, and the South Commission. Afterwards he became chair of the West Indian Commission (1992–94) (*Time for Action*) and co-chair of the Commission on Global Governance (1992–95) (*Our Global Neighbourhood*). He has also served as chancellor of the Universities of Guyana, Warwick and the West Indies. He was knighted in 1970 by the Queen, the Head of the Commonwealth.

Emeka Anyaoku (Nigeria) (1990–99) was born in 1933 and educated at University College of Ibadan, then part of the University of London. He joined the new ComSec in 1966 following appointments in CDC in London and Nigeria's Mission to the UN in New York. He was briefly Nigeria's foreign minister in 1983. He was SG in the immediate post-bipolar period when he could advance democratic governance empowered by the Harare Principles though election monitoring, good offices, membership suspensions, etc. His autobiography, *The Inside Story of the Modern Commonwealth*, was published by Evans in 2004. A chair was recently named in his honor at the Institute of Commonwealth Studies at the University of London. He is president of the WWF and of the Royal Commonwealth Society.

Don McKinnon (New Zealand) (1999–2007) had a 21-year career in New Zealand politics and government, much of it in international and regional affairs, before being elected fourth secretary-general at the Durban CHOGM. He is his country's longest serving minister of foreign affairs and trade—the decade of the 1990s—during which he was especially active on CMAG and around the small states agenda. As secretary-general he has advanced good governance and fair trade, reformed the administration of ComSec, entered into strategic alliances with other global agencies, and promoted small states.

The Secretariat expanded along with its membership and scope: the 1960s was the decade of African independence and the 1970s that of the Caribbean. Through the 1950s, the Commonwealth was but 10 percent of the UN; by the late 1980s it was approaching 30 percent, only to decline again to a quarter by century's turn given the proliferation of states in Central Europe and Central Asia with the end of the Cold War and the demise of the Soviet Union. And its focus likewise evolved, from decolonization to good governance through globalization and development and onto new security threats and responses like inter-communal dialogues.

Appropriately, the Commonwealths' expansion and inclusion of some 40 newly independent members in addition to those in South Asia was presided over by two secretaries-general from the South between those from Canada and New Zealand: Sonny Ramphal from Guyana (1975–90) and Emeka Anyaoku from Nigeria (1990–2000) (see Box 3.1). As Stephen Chan suggests, under the regime of the former, "Commonwealth influence reached its height, not only over Zimbabwe, but in international affairs generally."[1]

The Secretariat's size peaked at over 400 personnel in the mid-1980s, declining to 350 by the mid-1990s, around 300 by the new century and 250 by 2005. The Secretariat was restructured in the late 1960s and again in the 1990s, with the current secretary-general, Don McKinnon from New Zealand, instituting a controversial two-term rule for professional staff. By the middle of the first decade of the new century, ComSec advertisements for senior staff appeared regularly in the *Economist*, indicating the attraction and injection of new blood. Yet the administrative budget remains just over £10 million per annum (£13.5 million by mid-decade) despite inflation and the high cost of living in London, very much a cosmopolitan, world city.

All member states are represented on the Board of Governors of the Secretariat. But its 17-member Executive Committee includes the eight largest contributors—Australia, Canada, India, New Zealand, Nigeria, Singapore, South Africa and the UK—along with elected regional representatives. By 2005, the assessed budget included large and essential contributions from the UK (30 percent), Canada (19 percent), Australia (10 percent), South Africa (4 percent), India (3 percent), New Zealand (2 percent), etc. Members typically donate further sums for particular programs and projects.

The Secretariat's Strategic Plan and details of assessed contributions are now on the web along with its organizational plan. Likewise, its continually expanding website gives indications of how the twin goals of peace and democracy and pro-poor growth and sustainable development will be the responsibility of different divisions and programs (see Chapter 5 below). In addition to its own intra-Commonwealth resources and directions, ComSec increasingly seeks strategic alliances with compatible global agencies (e.g. *la francophonie* as well as the World Bank), regional organizations (e.g. AU, ECOWAS, EU, NEPAD, SADC) and individual states (e.g. Iceland and Norway) especially in its areas of focus like SIDS, trade, etc.

Following Marshall Aid as the catalyst for reconstruction in Europe, the Colombo Plan was created in January 1950 by the then new Commonwealth—Ceylon, India and Pakistan in addition to the three or four white Dominions—in response to decolonization in South Asia and the "communist threat" in Southeast Asia. This was an early consortium of bi- and multilateral agencies for Economic Development in South and Southeast Asia. It continues today in Sri Lanka as a modest secretariat in Colombo with a score staff yet under a somewhat expanded mandate—for Economic and Social Development in

Asia and the Pacific—with 25 members from Afghanistan to the Maldives and New Zealand, 11 of which are in the Commonwealth.

The new ComSec established its own Commonwealth Fund for Technical Cooperation (CFTC) in the early 1970s, and this has also remained modest: £1 million in 1973, peaking at £25 million in the late 1980s, declining to 20 million per annum at century's turn, rising slightly to £24 million in 2005. Rather than capital, infrastructural funds, it specializes in the provision of technical or functional assistance, especially South-South; some 100 to 500 experts each year. Despite superior leadership from Mike Faber and a positive evaluation by John Toye in the mid-1990s, given its functional focus it has always been rather marginal compared to bilateral official development assistance (ODA) via the Development Assistance Committee (DAC) in the OECD as well as multilateral assistance from the UN and IFIs and now the expanding EU. Its own annual report in 2006 emphasized a set of goals related to Commonwealth values and the MDGs which overlap with those of some other Commonwealth agencies: sharing expertise; enhancing trade and competitiveness; managing debt and accessing finance; supporting sustainable development and pro-poor policies; strengthening the public sector; advancing education and health; and promoting democracy and the rule of law. The largest contributors to date to the CFTC in the twenty-first century have been: Australia, Canada, India, New Zealand, Nigeria, Singapore, South Africa, and the UK, reflective of their OECD, NIC and/or BRIC (or BRICSA) status/aspirations.

Following the early absorption of ten or twelve functional agencies in the late 1960s, ComSec settled into a set of programs broadly divided into political, developmental, social and central or institutional, the latter being Secretariat governance, strategic planning and CHOGM preparations and executions. As we saw in the previous chapter, the 1960s were preoccupied with decolonization, primarily in Sub-Saharan Africa, and the 1970s and 1980s by the anti-apartheid struggle in Southern Africa. The post-bipolar, post-apartheid 1990s were dominated by questions of good governance as the Harare Principles were agreed and then elaborated and effected. So the Secretariat's agenda expanded from decolonization and small states to include regime and election monitoring as well as the absorption of two somewhat atypical new members in 1995: Cameroon and Mozambique. For a comprehensive insider's account spanning 34 years of the four decades in Marlborough House— i.e. most of these transitions—including a decade as secretary-general from 1990 to 2000, with an emphasis on personal diplomacy, see Emeka Anyaoku's autobiography[2] (see also Box 3.1).

By 2005, ComSec comprised two deputy secretaries-general (DSGs) and a dozen divisions, each with a director as indicated in Figure 3.1. The Secretary-General's Office had a couple of divisions reporting to it: Communications and Public Affairs and Strategic Planning and Evaluation. In turn, one DSG was responsible for "economic" matters—Economic Affairs, Governance and Institutional Development, Social Transformation and Advisory Service—the other DSG for "political"—Political, Legal and Constitutional, Human Rights, Corporate and Youth (the last with its own budget of some £2.5 million per annum now including its own biennial summit at CHOGM). At

Figure 3.1 Commonwealth Secretariat structure.

the start of 2007, the pair of deputy secretaries-general were Ransford Smith (Jamaica) and Florence Mugaisha (Uganda), respectively.

Amongst the innovative forms of contracting-out of diplomatic services has been the development of the secretary-general's "good offices" role. Conceptually, special envoys can be located between non-controversial election-monitoring on the one hand and, on the other, high politics around CMAG consideration possibly leading to suspension. As the number of members has grown along with expectations about democratic processes, the frequency and range as well as delicacy of such diplomatic missions has grown: from pre-emptive to crisis management. They constitute a low-level type of diplomatic intervention: "responsibility to protect" (R2P) populations from ineffective or oppressive regimes.

In November 2006, Don McKinnon brought a set of current envoys together to consider how to develop and exploit such roles to advance communication, conflict resolution, democracy, development and peace given emerging policy challenges and diplomatic competitors in the new century. Such eminent Commonwealth persons included General Abubakar and Adebayo Adedeji of Nigeria, Joe Clark and Christine Stewart of Canada and others. They were to be joined by Ibrahim Gambari of Nigeria and Lakhdar Brahimi of Algeria *inter alia* who have been active in non-Commonwealth, UN contexts. Such personalities tend to have had administrative, legal or political roles at national, regional or global levels. As with the eminence of recent Expert Groups and Commissions, so the Secretariat's ability to secure the expensive services of such eminent persons is reflective of the high regard with which it is held. To date, unlike some of the UN agencies, the Commonwealth has not appointed continuing special representatives or ambassadors, such as Ronaldo (Brazil), Zinedine Zidane (France) and Nadine Gordimer (RSA) for UNDP; Bono and the EU and MDGs; Geldof and the G8/Live 8, etc., as analyzed by Andrew Cooper in his forthcoming *Celebrity Diplomacy*.[3]

By century's end, the Commonwealth was focused on globalization and governance in addition to the continued privileging of small states and functional services (see comparative analysis of a set of turn-of-the-century reports on the Commonwealths' futures in the concluding chapter below). Thus between Brisbane and Abuja, a Commonwealth Expert Group, with India's Manmohan Singh as chair, deliberated on the nexus between democracy and development. This report brought together many of the best thinkers in state and non-state agencies and think-tanks in the Commonwealths, maintaining the Commonwealths' well deserved reputation for creative analysis and advocacy, which

more than equals that of the larger UN system.[4] Its salience has subsequently been reinforced by its chair's elevation to the prime minis-
tership in India, the only Commonwealth member of the four BRIC
emerging economies. I return to its significance for the Commonwealths and global governance in the final chapter on the future.

As already noted, aside from endless informal interaction including
the biennial CHOGM/CPF juxtaposition, the inter- and non-state
Commonwealths in Marlborough House are brought together by the
civil society liaison officer (50 percent ComSec; 50 percent Foundation),
presently David Kalete from Uganda.

Foundation

If ComSec is a minnow, then the parallel Commonwealth Foundation
is miniscule: a dozen staff and budget of just £3 million to advance
civil society throughout the extended family. On its establishment four
decades ago, the Foundation was to enhance the development of
nongovernmental professional associations, some of which preceded
both Commonwealths. Although a voluntary intergovernmental body
itself—only some three-quarters of the Commonwealth's member
states subscribe (presently 46 after the welcome accession of South
Africa in late 2006 plus one Associate: Gibraltar)—it has spearheaded
the development and recognition of the approximately 70 professional
associations and then myriad NGOs in civil society throughout and
beyond the Commonwealth (see Appendix 3). These now participate
in the biennial parallel Commonwealth People's Forum (CPF) to the
CHOGM. And the Foundation awards almost 100 modest grants each
year to civil society organizations. But its marginal budget of a quarter million pounds at birth in 1965, half a million by 1975 and £1
million in the 1980s passed £2 million in the early 1990s and £2.5
million by the end of the century. Its energetic new leadership in the
middle of the first decade of the new century seeks further funds and
members as it focuses attention on a trio of areas as indicated below.

As the status of "global" civil society has grown around the turn of
the century, so the Foundation's purview has broadened beyond
established professional associations to NGOs and CBOs, reflected in
its turn-of-the-century project and publications on civil society in the
new millennium ahead of the planned Brisbane CPF (NB there was
no simultaneous CHOGM for first time in late 2001 as such timing was
disrupted by 9/11): *Citizens and Governance* in the several regions of
the Commonwealth.[5] Two years later, in Abuja, it orchestrated a meeting on development and democracy, the theme of the Manmohan Singh

EG, with an emphasis on Africa, especially Nigeria, including a dialogue with the secretary-general.[6] This brought voices from throughout the Commonwealths' several regions—seven meetings of over 150 civil society representatives from over 45 member countries between May and December 2003—including the first-ever consultation between ComSec and Foundation networks in London before the COW in November 2003. These were reinforced by some 70 civil society representatives at the CPF. Commonwealth civil society called on CHOGM and CPF to advance human development, human rights and human security. It welcomed

> the Heads of Government endorsement at their last meeting (at Coolum in 2002) of "a Commonwealth known, owned and valued by its peoples, responsive to their evolving needs, and invigorated by a more focused and productive partnership between governments and civil society."
> ... We believe that the Commonwealth—with its principles and stated values, diverse global membership, and collaborative framework—could make the significant contribution to such a world ... but only if its principles were to be more closely matched by its practice.[7]

Similarly, Foundation staff again, but with CSAC for the first time, organized a series of consultations leading towards the summit in Malta at the end of 2005: "From Local to Global: a Commonwealth experiment in strengthening global governance and engaging citizens." In mid-decade, it also undertook an inter-regional consultation on the MDGs: "Breaking with Business as Usual: perspectives from civil society in the Commonwealth on the MDGs." Its programming is presently divided into a trio of sections reflective of contemporary civil society emphases: governance and democracy, sustainable development, and culture and diversity. In turn, its structure has come to recognize and incorporate the informal Commonwealth.

Table 3.1 Selected Commonwealth NGOs

Bangladesh	BRAC, Grameen
Britain	Aga Khan Foundation, Amnesty International, Oxfam, SCF, VSO
Canada	CUSO
India	PRIA
South Africa	Civicus, IDASA, TRAC

As discussed in previous chapters, a Civil Society Advisory Committee (CSAC) was first appointed in 1999: a representative, eminent group of 10 (1999–2003) then 16 (2004–7) leading indigenous and international NGO activists and think-tank analysts from the several regions of the Commonwealth: Africa, Asia, Caribbean and the Pacific, etc. Since 2004 it has had representatives on the Foundation's Board, which otherwise consists of high commissioners of member states in London and, as noted above, it facilitated the organization and implementation of the CPF in Malta in November 2005. It is likewise animating a series of pre-CPF events in Uganda in the year preceding the Kampala CHOGM in November 2007, where its CPF theme is "Transforming Commonwealth Societies." The Foundation also organizes an annual training workshop for new appointees in High Commissions in London to facilitate their multi- as well as bilateral roles.

While the Secretariat and Foundation have symbolized the two sides of the Commonwealths in Marlborough House in the heart of ex-imperial London for over four decades, on the west coast of Canada is now to be found a relatively new and innovative Commonwealth agency reflective of the Commonwealths as global networks around sectors like education: COL, established in Vancouver in 1987.

Commonwealth of Learning

The Commonwealths have always been concerned about education as well as communication, development and health, as is reflected in the well established ACU, specialized League for Exchange of Commonwealth Teachers (LECT) and recent Consortium for Commonwealth Education (CfCE) amongst others. Indeed, before hosting ComSec, Marlborough House was in part a hub for such post-war Commonwealth educational networks.

Given an expanding membership, especially small island states, and changes in communications technologies, CHOGM at Vancouver in 1987 decided to create a COL in British Columbia to advance distance education at all levels. It is the only intergovernmental agency devoted to the promotion and delivery of distance education and open learning knowledge resources and technologies. This decision was based on earlier deliberations at the 1985 Nassau summit and a report from a working group chaired by Asa Briggs, who had been associated with new post-war universities in Britain like Sussex and the Open University (OU) as well as compiling the multi-volume history of the BBC, arguably the empire's greatest contribution and legacy, especially as it becomes both global and digital. COL has been connected to a database at the OU, one of its many educational partners. It also links with relevant agencies in the UN system like UNESCO, WHO and WIPO and Commonwealth-centric regional organizations like CAR-ICOM, ECOWAS and SADC: one of David Armstrong's "network of networks."[8]

At the turn of the century, COL had come to focus on the MDGs and Education for All, along with Commonwealth values. It now has an annual budget of some C$10 million, with its major donors being Canada, India, New Zealand, Nigeria, South Africa and the UK. They all have seats on its Board along with four regional representatives from around the Commonwealth. It has some 45 staff who concentrate on aspects of education, technology, sustainability, etc. Among its recent foci has been a proposal to create a virtual university for some 25 small states of the Commonwealth. In its current 2006–9 three-year plan—*Learning for Development*—approved by 16CCEM in Cape Town in December 2006, COL aims to maintain its focus on global development, including South-South, but to concentrate on longer-term partnerships. As its current president, Sir John Daniel, who was previously associated with OU and UNESCO as well as with Canadian universities and COL, wrote in his "Foreword" to the latest plan:

> Expanding human learning is essential to the achievement of every element in this agenda and knowledge is the road to freedom. Conventional teaching methods cannot cope with the scale of the challenge, but technology—old and new—harnessed to aid learning and share knowledge can.[9]

Commonwealth Business Council

Economic as well as political liberalization intensified in the final decade of the last century, following the fall of the Berlin Wall. This new context permitted the Commonwealth as well as the UN to reach out beyond member states to the private sector as well as civil society. The UN Global Compact was launched at the turn of the century. And the last leg of the Commonwealth "stool" was likewise instituted in the late 1990s—1997 in Edinburgh—to advance globalization for all through good governance, social responsibility, enhanced investment, increased trade and improved technologies. Analysis of the benefits for the business sector arising from association with the anglophone Commonwealth suggests that such trade and investment gain from a

10–15 percent Commonwealth factor or bonus. This is the advantage which arises from efficiencies of business amongst partner states and companies, technologies and consumers with broadly similar institutions and expectations as well as language.[10]

The Commonwealth Business Council (CBC) brings together over 200 of the Commonwealth's leading companies, especially from Australia, Canada, India, South Africa and the UK (see Table 3.2), and some 4,000 associate members. Its interests reflect those of the IFIs, OECD, EU, BRICs, business associations, etc.: corporate social responsibility (CSR), consulting, corruption, dialogue, gender, globalization, governance, investment, networking, technology and tri-sectoral partnerships. All of these display an emphasis on Africa, especially Nigeria and South Africa, the Caribbean, South and Southeast Asia (especially India as a BRIC and Singapore as a NIC) and the South Pacific. Commonwealth economies are amongst the most globalized, according to the *Foreign Policy* and A. T. Kearney "globalization index" calculated each year, with Singapore being highly ranked along with the ABC countries. But the top 60 states usually also include others like Botswana, India, Malaysia, South Africa and Uganda.

The CBC has a very active set of events to advance such links in every region of the Commonwealth: over 30 between April 2003 and the November 2005 CHOGM, especially in Africa and India as well as London. Its Management Board includes globally recognized Commonwealth entrepreneurs like Rahul Bajaj (India), Lakshimi Mittal (UK) and Cyril Ramaphosa (South Africa). Its report for the Commonwealth Business Forum around CHOGM in Malta at the end of 2005 was on "Making Globalization Work for All: achievements and prospects." It included mention of benefits or bonuses arising from the Commonwealth factor, already noted, of common language, legal systems, administrative procedures and political outlook: "the 'Commonwealth factor' makes doing business by one Commonwealth country with another at least 15 percent cheaper than between non-Commonwealth countries."

Table 3.2 Selected Commonwealth MNCs

Australia	ANZ Banking, BHP Billiton, News Corporation, Telstra
Britain	Barclays, BG, BP, Shell, Unilever
Canada	Alcan, Barrack, Talisman, Petro-Canada
India	Birla, Indian Oil, Reliance, State Bank, Tata
South Africa	Anglo American, De Beers, Gold Fields, MTN, SABMiller

The assertion of a positive Commonwealth economic factor has been further developed through a Canadian-centered innovation—"Commonwealth Advantage"—which seeks to exploit anglophone Commonwealth high-tech connections, including professional mobility, particularly around South Asia. It advocates and advances the benefits of the Commonwealth factor through myriad discussions about branding, mobility, networking, trade, technology, etc. Reflective of contemporary, especially anglophone, Anglo-American predispositions, Commonwealth corporations and civil societies are increasingly communicating and collaborating around issues of social responsibility rather than accepting or even encouraging antagonism.

Civil society

The Commonwealth, emulating the example of the British empire, has always had a dynamic nongovernmental dimension, in addition to a variety of Christian missionaries, as indicated by the anti-slavery and free trade movements which date back to the eighteenth and nineteenth centuries. So Anti-Slavery International (ASI) can claim to be the world's oldest human rights organization. And the earliest "Commonwealth" nongovernmental institutions—professional associations—concentrated in education, media and politics, preceded World War I: CPU (1909), CPA (1911), and ACU (1913) (see Appendix 3).

In many ways, as suggested already, the Commonwealths' influence is a function of pragmatic and productive established divisions of labor between Marlborough House, on the one hand, and the professional associations and civil society, on the other; i.e. the inter- and non-state Commonwealths. The latter are concentrated in the developmental, educational, gender, governance, health, legal, media, political and professional sectors, but they span the spectrum of organizational life. Many of the Commonwealths' activities are performed by its approximately 70 professional institutions with minimal direction or regulation from either Secretariat or Foundation. These are increasingly balanced by a less recognized set of civil society groupings or NGOs: Commonwealth Plus. As already noted, some of the former predate the post-imperial Commonwealth and some are listed and briefly described in Appendix 3.[11]

Some of these Associations and NGOs are more controversial than others: for example, those concerned with human rights and indigenous peoples (Commonwealth Human Rights Initiative (CHRI) and Commonwealth Association of Indigenous Peoples (CAIP)) (on the latter, see the final paragraph in this section) versus, say, the rather venerable Commonwealth Parliamentary Association (CPA) or Royal Commonwealth Society (RCS), the latter treated in the next paragraph. And some Commonwealth Plus NGOs are less recognized in or rarely claim association with the Commonwealths *per se* (e.g. AKF, BRAC or WWF versus, say, PRIA, Oxfam or VSO?) (see Table 3.1 above).

The Royal Commonwealth Society (RCS) is the oldest formal Commonwealth civil society network (see ASI), dating back to 1868. It belatedly evolved out of the white Dominions toward a global network and now offers a broad range of programming in London and elsewhere, stretching from multi-culturalism to confidence-building, especially the annual Commonwealth Day (second Monday of March) events. The latter now includes a CD-ROM for schools on the annual theme, such as "Health and Vitality: the Commonwealth challenge" in March 2006 to tie into that month's Melbourne Games or "Respecting Difference and Promoting Understanding" in March 2007 to publicize the Commonwealths' new concern and Commission. On the latter occasion, for the first time Uganda so celebrated, six months ahead of hosting CHGOM.

Symbolically, the London RCS Commonwealth Club on Northumberland Avenue between Trafalgar Square and the Thames has undergone a revolution from stuffy club with dingy albeit homey library to modern meeting space with *nouvelle cuisine.* It now sports a strategic alliance with the neighboring Citadines hotel along with a continuing connection with the Royal Overseas League with its own residential facilities adjoining neighboring Green Park. The most recent expansion of its facilities, with a handsome new entrance looking up to Trafalgar Square and the several Commonwealth high commissions located around it (i.e. Canadian, South African and Ugandan with that of Nigeria across the street on Northumberland Avenue), was opened in mid-2006. Even before the latter, McIntyre had asserted that "the RCS re-established itself as a premier forum for discussion about the Commonwealth."[12]

In turn, ComSec, having metamorphosed, butterfly-like, out of a few Commonwealth functional agencies already located in Marlborough House, has itself served as incubator of several new agencies, some of which have become free-standing or semi-detached over time. These have evolved from functional agencies like the Commonwealth Agricultural Bureaux (CAB-International from 1986)—with research networks and institutes in the regions of the Commonwealth in addition to the UK, intended to protect food chains originating in the tropics—which was spun-off as a formally post-Commonwealth CABI in the late 1990s.[13] It presently has 45 members, 5 of which are OTs and 12 of which are outside both Commonwealth and OT networks. As a not-for-profit global agency, it hosts bioscience centers in Britain and Switzerland, and in China, Kenya, Malaysia, Pakistan and Trinidad; and has a very active publications program of research abstracts and books, with its 15 journals now being published by Cambridge University Press. As McIntyre concludes, "Over the span of 80 years, a colonial pest identification service has grown to be a world leader in information science, scientific publishing and ecological health."[14] Similarly, the functions of the Commonwealth Telecommunications Board were absorbed by CTO, treated below.

And new tasks, related to novel governance and technological directions and opportunities, have led to new agencies such as the Commonwealth of Learning (1987), already noted above, Commonwealth Association for Public Administration (CAPAM) and Commonwealth Local Government Forum (CLGF) (both created in 1994) plus the Commonwealth Business Council (1997), mentioned already in this chapter. Given cutbacks, ComSec favors one umbrella organization for each sector to which it can relate (e.g. CCfE for the educational sector).

Finally, as a segue from civil society to human rights, I mention one area in which the Commonwealths, notwithstanding their achievements around ending colonialism and racist rule in Southern Africa, have come up short: that of recognizing and advancing indigenous communities. The Commonwealths' approximately 2 billion population includes some 150 million indigenous peoples in a majority of member states, but concentrated in Australia, Botswana, Canada, India, New Zealand, etc. Such indigenous communities tend to be marginal—with lower indicators for education, health, housing, human rights, income, etc.—as indicated in the title of a 2003 report by Richard Bourne "Invisible Lives: undercounted, underrepresented and underneath: the socio-economic plight of indigenous peoples in the Commonwealth." Increasingly, they have come to be organized regionally (e.g. around the Arctic and Pacific) and globally. And some federal and state governments in, say, Australia, Canada and New Zealand, have adopted relatively enlightened policies and practices, albeit under pressure.

But Commonwealth states as a whole have been peculiarly reluctant to recognize and treat indigenous peoples as a distinct set of communities, despite progress toward recognition and support in the UN. And Commonwealth civil society has not advanced their cause as much as, say, majority rule in Southern Africa, sustainable development, human rights, etc. Moreover, to date, despite encouragement from CHRI (see next section), the Commonwealth Association of Indigenous Peoples (CAIP), launched at the Durban CHOGM in 1999, has not received much attention or support.[15]

Human rights

The intergovernmental Commonwealth animated by Sonny Ramphal as secretary-general (see Box 3.1 above) was in the vanguard of the global anti-apartheid movement in the 1970s and 1980s. The non-state Commonwealths have always included professional associations and related NGOs which advocated human rights, a position which became more familiar as the Cold War drew to a close. As the Commonwealths' extended family enlarged its anti-racism preoccupation toward a broader concern for social rights, five, then seven or eight professional associations came together to advance the Commonwealth Human Rights Initiative (CHRI); namely, initially, CJA, CLA, CLEA, CMA and the Commonwealth Trades Union Council (CTUC), then also CPA and CPU, with CBA also signing up later. The Initiative concentrates on access to information, including constitutionalism and access to justice, especially reform of police and prisons. Its headquarters of some 50 staff is in New Delhi, with smaller offices in Accra and London. CHRI has been supported by the Ford and Tata foundations, the New Zealand and UK governments and the Foundation.

The first report from the CHRI was prepared for the Harare CHOGM at the start of the post-bipolar era: "Put our World to Rights." It has drafted and launched reports at each subsequent biennial CHOGM, most recently on the right to information and on the right to good policing. And it has been supportive of the definition and implementation of the Harare Principles, including suspension of offending member states. For instance, it undertook a fact-finding mission to Nigeria during that country's darkest period of military rule in the mid-1990s, so supporting the suspension of the military regime. CHRI has consistently advocated ComSec recognition of such rights and appropriate capacity to effect them, though its support for a stand-alone Human Rights Unit in the Secretariat has never been effective. But not all member states are enamored of such persistent advocacy of a cosmopolitan conception of human rights.

A similar, compatible, jointly supported initiative was developed after the Harare Principles began to be defined and implemented by several of the original instigators of the CHRI. The CLA, CLEA, CMJA and CPA met in June 1998 at Latimer House outside London to draw up the "Latimer House Guidelines." Their focus was not on

24-hour news service on cable and satellite TV as well as online: a crucial dimension of Britain's "public diplomacy" along with the British Council and ESU, but one that is increasingly global rather than national. However, conversely, the global role played by British secondary school examination bodies—the London and Oxbridge universities examination boards—has largely disappeared as the UK educational sector has been reformed and rendered more competitive or commercial, though the Cambridge board is still active. Their role of global monitoring and mobility has been largely replaced by the less Commonwealth-centric but largely anglophone International Baccalaureate (IB) out of Geneva. I turn in the final section of this chapter to the several strands in Commonwealth Plus around the broad field of communication.

Global communication

Just as the British empire was based on good communication—from thin red line of the Royal Navy and merchant shipping to early telecommunications via Cable and Wireless and others—so the Commonwealths have encouraged and exploited anglophone links. I highlight four well established and regarded associations in this sector before turning to major Commonwealth literary organizations and awards and a trio of Commonwealth-centric journals in conclusion. I return to the Commonwealths and global futures in the final chapter.

Meanwhile, reflective of technological change, the first such professional association was for the printed page: the Commonwealth Press Union (CPU) founded in the first decade of the twentieth century turns 100 in 2009. It now embraces 750 newspaper and agency members, producing 1,500 newspapers in 49 states and focuses on freedom of the press, advancing Commonwealth values and training and facilities for media professionals. Second, the Commonwealth Broadcasting Association (CBA) was established at the end of World War II and has expanded from radio to television. It publishes an annual "Broadcaster Directory" and has over a hundred members from the broadcasting sector with a concentration on public broadcasting. And third, the Commonwealth Journalists' Association (CJA) was established in 1978 to advance and defend journalists and their profession. It has members throughout the Commonwealth and is presently located in Trinidad and Tobago.

Finally, the Commonwealth Telecommunications Organization (CTO) is a major network of Commonwealth and other state and private telecommunications providers and manufacturers. Although it started at the beginning of the twentieth century with fixed phone lines, it has become more diverse and engaged in the twenty-first century, advancing IT, mobile telecommunications and the Internet. It used to integrate the empire. Now it seeks to overcome the digital divide and advance the MDGs though technical cooperation. The CTO supports the independent regulation of telecoms and ICTs in a post-nationalization era, seeking to advance commercialization and privatization of telecommunications for development. It receives support from 35 Commonwealth countries who sit on its Board; i.e. three-quarters of the present membership of ComSec.

Given global trends toward ICTs as well as its own place between Europe and Africa, as well as being a new member of the EU, as host of the late-2005 CHOGM, Malta took as its theme, "Networking the Commonwealth for Development" (see the Malta Communiqué in Appendix 4). In turn, both CHOGM and CPF adopted and adapted the networking motif for their own purposes; the secretary-general's annual report for 2005 was on "Networking for Progress and Prosperity" and the CPF focus in Malta was "Networking Commonwealth People." And as already indicated in Chapter 1, one legacy of the Malta summit is a new ICT program, "Commonwealth Connects," supported by India, Mozambique, and Trinidad and Tobago as well as Malta.

The Commonwealth Writer's Prize for fiction was established in 1987 as Commonwealth/post-colonial literature became well established, and is administered by the Commonwealth Foundation. It now offers ten prizes per annum—half for best book, the other half for best first book—through four sets of regional awards and one global, selected from the regional winners. Winners over the last two decades have included some increasingly eminent authors, reflective of Commonwealth diversity, such as Peter Carey (Australia), Austin Clarke (Canada), J. M. Coetzee (South Africa), Rohinton Mistry (Canada) and Zadie Smith (UK). In 2006, at presentations in Melbourne to coincide with the Commonwealth Games, the Best Book award went to Kate Grenville (Australia) for *The Secret River* and Best First Book to Mark McWatt (Guyana) for *Suspended Sentences: fictions of atonement.*

The global Association for Commonwealth Literature and Language Studies (ACLALS) is a very extensive set of networks bringing together academics, writers, reviewers, editors and media in a triennial conference. It was launched at Leeds in 1964 and its next triennial meeting is in Vancouver in mid-August 2007. It has nine chapters in Canada, Europe, India, South Pacific and the West Indies, including the United States. It sits at the borders of the extended Commonwealth family and broader anglophone post-colonial studies networks, largely in language, culture and history, as indicated in the discussion of Commonwealth studies in the next chapter.

There are many uni- and inter-disciplinary journals connected to the Commonwealth, national and regional as well as global, but arguably the two or three best known in the social sciences and history are *Round Table*, founded in 1910, *Commonwealth and Comparative Politics*, established just over 40 years ago, and *The Journal of Imperial and Commonwealth History* all now published by Routledge in the UK. Tables of contents and article abstracts for all three are now online and many university libraries offer online editions for their global subscribers.

Round Table claims in its subtitle to be *The Commonwealth Journal of International Affairs*. When it was launched before World War I, it was indeed *the* definitive such journal of record, reflective of contemporary policy thinking in London about empire. But, as the imperial project became more problematic between the wars under pressure from skeptical Labour ginger groups, it lost its cachet. Peter Lyon at the Institute of Commonwealth Studies valiantly maintained its niche in the traditional discipline of "international relations" for two decades at the end of the twentieth century when IR could still claim to be authoritative—a special issue was dedicated to him in September 2004 on "Commonwealth Perspectives" with contributions from leading Commonwealth figures as well as eminent scholars of international relations like James Mayall, Tony Payne and Jennifer Welsh— and Andrew Williams, now at St. Andrews, has injected new energy and connections in its ninth post-bipolar/post-realist decade. It is now appears six times a year, with occasional special issues, such as those on the "Commonwealth at 40" in July 2005 and on religion, conflict and conflict resolution in October 2005. It has regular dinner meetings and discussions in London, and editorial boards also meet at each CHOGM/CPF, as in Malta in late 2005 and Kampala in late 2007.

After each CHOGM/CPF, *Round Table* holds a reflective discussion with major stakeholders, usually at Cumberland Lodge (see previous section), the reports of which appear on its own webpage, which also lists some of the histories of the journal and its parallel think-tank activities. In January 2007 it carried a set of reflections in response to the critical Srinivasan book on *The Rise, Decline and Future of the British Commonwealth*.[19] Its distinctive dimensions have included a comprehensive "Commonwealth Update," which Derek Ingram generated for many decades and excellent "Commonwealth Bookshelf" and book reviews edited by Terry Barringer. It anticipates a series of commemorative debates and publications around its centenary in 2009/2010 reflecting on its academic and applied contributions to discipline and network.

Commonwealth and Comparative Politics is not as well established or establishment as *Round Table*, but is nevertheless well regarded in the field of comparative politics, especially that of the South and rest of the Commonwealth. It appears thrice a year, with occasional special issues. Ahead of its 40th birthday, the last issue of volume 39 in November 2001 was a special one of 160 pages on "The Commonwealth in Comparative Perspective."[20] And *The Journal of Imperial and Commonwealth History* now appears each quarter. Its last special issue at the start of 2006 was on "Empire and Monarchy."

Both Commonwealth literature institutions and this trio of journals advance interdisciplinary Commonwealth studies, as treated below in Chapter 4 along with issues around the Commonwealths and pro- and anti-globalization discourses.

4 Commonwealths' discourses and directions

Pro- and/or anti-globalizations

If the Commonwealth does have a future as a thriving and relevant IGO, it is probably through some combination of ... "re-inventions": small states, good governance and globalization.

(David Armstrong)[1]

... rather than being trapped in the past, the Commonwealth is acquiring a new significance in the modern world by virtue of its unique network qualities. It embraces nations across the globe, rich and poor, large and small. And its members are linked by countless linguistic, cultural, sporting, family and business ties.

(Ruth Lea)[2]

This chapter provides a transition from the more institutional and historical to the more virtual and contemporary Commonwealths, those of "extended families" as indicated by Ruth Lea's words above. After examining the Commonwealths and governance, it focuses on the Commonwealths and globalization as well as pro- and anti-globalization debates, which hold applied as well as analytic implications given my assumption or assertion that the Commonwealths are distinctive by being closely connected to many aspects of contemporary globalization nexuses or syndromes. It also identifies and highlights Commonwealth-related "global" issues like migrations, diasporas and remittances, and small (island) states, features of Armstrong's trio of possible reinventions of the Commonwealths quoted above. It then contrasts Commonwealth and global studies, two overlapping fields of analysis. In the following, penultimate chapter, I concentrate on Commonwealth Plus; i.e. "external" yet relevant and related aspects of the Commonwealths' civil societies and international companies in world politics.

Commonwealths and governance: how good?

Momentum toward global governance accelerated at the end of the Cold War as the number of global actors and global issues multiplied, in part as spill-overs from the uneven incidence and impacts of "early" globalization. There are many definitions of "globalizations," which I pluralize to indicate multiple features, emphasizing particular analytic, historical and existential positions. But I take their characteristics to be multidimensional, uneven, even unanticipated; ideological as well as institutional, generating a variety of governance challenges and responses. To be sure, the British and other empires, including Oriental as well as European ones, constituted earlier "imperial" forms of globalization whose legacies linger in myriad diasporas, mining investments, etc. As one of the leading students of globalization, Jan Aart Scholte, admits: "academic knowledge of globalization not only has intellectual significance, but political consequence as well."[3]

Contemporary Commonwealth networks *per se* are not central to globalizations, yet because of their linguistic, professional content, they are not irrelevant either; they both augment and moderate cultural, technical and personal dimensions. They may also be taken to be interesting, idiosyncratic cases of political and social if not so much economic or structural globalizations: the post-industrial, information or network political economy. Thus they may contribute even if unintentionally and unwittingly to a more nuanced inclusive, inter-disciplinary—cosmopolitan?—conceptualization of globalizations. As Jan Aart Scholte indicates himself, at least in his second edition, the Commonwealth along with the UN and IFIs is one of a few "prominent examples of governance bodies with global remit."[4]

But tensions in the last decade of the twentieth century between pro- and anti-globalization forces intensified around the series of symbolic EU, G8 and WTO summits—but not biennial CHOGMs—culminating in the "Battle of Seattle" over the proposed MAI in 1999. The Canadian Halifax G8 summit in 1995 may have been peaceful; those following in Evian and Gleneagles, etc., were not. In mid-decade, governments like that of Canada sought publicity for the G8; thereafter they attempted to minimize any such popular antagonistic attention by locating summits in rural sites like Kananaskis and Sea Island. But anti- or alter-globalization networks like Attac and No Logo continued to encourage opposition to corporate globalization with more representative intergovernmental agencies like the ILO and Commonwealth attempting to put a positive spin on the benefits as well as costs of globalization: "fair" and "people-centered," respectively.

But, as the United States is not a member and the UK is no longer a hegemonic global power—as Srinivasan laments in his 2005 book, the latter is hardly interested in or supportive of today's Commonwealth—should the Commonwealths be leading targets of transatlantic anti-globalization attention? The Commonwealths gain a degree of freedom of maneuver without the United States as a member state. Further, they may again realize a level of influence in the new century because

- they now include a BRIC as well as NIC(s);
- their nongovernmental networks continue to be innovative, relevant, and engaged; and
- as indicated in the first chapter, other post-imperial Commonwealths lack the same degree of cohesion, diversity and direction of relevance to contemporary globalizations.

Moreover, the Commonwealths have recently begun to transcend their disinterest in "security," as it is coming to be redefined in ways which are more compatible with their historic concerns with human development and democratic communities.

Commonwealths and new and human security

The post-bipolar pattern of pro- and anti-globalization stand-offs established in the 1990s was shattered at the start of the twenty-first century by the terrorist attacks on the Twin Towers in New York on 9/11, which were subsequently reinforced by the London mass transit bombs on 7/7. This served to divert anti-globalization networks while at least initially advancing a narrow "national security" definition of pro-globalization: the United States-defined "war on terrorism." As Marlies Glasius *et al.* suggested in the second annual edition of *Global Civil Society 2002*:

> On 10 September 2001, the day before the attacks on New York and Washington, the phenomenon that we call "global civil society" was flourishing ... characterised by the growing importance attached to global norms and values—human rights, the environment, social justice—which were beginning to displace the geo-political discourse of international affairs ...
> So what was the impact of September 11 ... and of October 7, the day the air strikes against Afghanistan began?
> ... These two events could be understood as the moment at which global civil society comes of age.[5]

Such rapid maturation became even more compelling in mid-decade, especially in Britain and the Commonwealths. In the post-war era, both had facilitated mobility, diversity and communication, yet the subsequent mid-decade London suicide bombers of 7/7 belonged to families from the Commonwealths' post-World War II diasporas in the UK. These mid-2005 terrorist attacks in central London, coinciding with the Scottish G8 summit at Gleneagles, served as a further catalyst for reconsideration of the Commonwealths' avoidance to date of "security." That issue had been taken to be the responsibility of other international organizations like NATO and the OSCE. But such established inter-agency divisions of labor reflect earlier bipolar formulations of "national" rather than "human" security. And they apparently failed to anticipate or contain "new" security threats from alienated, radicalized "Islamic" youth so their reputations became somewhat tarnished and popular confidence in them diminished. Hence, reinforced by increasingly problematic wars in Iraq and Afghanistan, definitions of and responses to novel security challenges encouraged innovative policy and institutional responses in the second half of the decade, more compatible with established yet not inflexible Commonwealth inclinations and interests.

With the passing of the glory days of their epistemic role in the overthrow of minority rule in Southern Africa treated in Chapter 2 above, the Commonwealths were in search of a new purpose post-apartheid as well as post-bipolarity. At the start of the twenty-first century, challenged by 9/11 and 7/7, where do the Commonwealths stand in regard to contemporary security? The continuing metamorphosis of the "war on terrorism" and the conflicts in Afghanistan and Iraq may yet lead to another opportunity for the Commonwealths and other agencies not traditionally concerned about inter-state conflict containment or peace-building: to advance human security as well as human development and human rights through inter-community and inter-faith communication and dialogue, especially in multi-cultural and multi-religious member countries like Britain, Canada, India, Nigeria, and so on.

Unfortunately, by postponing CHOGM in Brisbane immediately following 9/11 the intergovernmental Commonwealth missed an early opportunity to carve out such a creative or courageous role. However, between the subsequent mid-decade Malta and Uganda summits, it has become so engaged around the respect and understanding agenda at both inter- and non-state levels, as indicated in Appendix 4's Malta Communiqué. I treat emerging Foundation programming and ComSec deliberations toward the end of Chapter 5. These now include a novel

Commonwealth Commission on respect and understanding chaired by Amartya Sen, reflective of his earlier role at century's turn as co-chair with Sadako Ogata of the Independent Commission on Human Security. Such informed deliberations are compatible with the identification of a middle ground by the Commonwealths and other pragmatic inter- and non-state agencies in parallel debates about humane globalization and human security.

The Commonwealths are in part a result of earlier, imperial globalizations which generated a set of enlightened professional associations as well as regressive racism in Southern Africa and elsewhere. Notwithstanding their anti-colonial genesis, reflective of the hegemony of the so-called "Washington Consensus," at least until the dawn of the twenty-first century, they have long since abandoned any anti-globalization inclinations rather than alter-globalization or humane globalization. So Armstrong can suggest that it has become "an IGO well suited for an era of globalization. The 1999 CHOGM issued a special declaration on Globalization and People-Centred Development which pointed to the problems globalization posed for poorer countries."[6] The Commonwealths, non- as well as inter-state, tend to advance a form of reformist globalization largely compatible with the ILO-supported World Commission on the Social Dimensions of Globalization—"A Fair Globalization"—which, like human development and human security, focuses on people rather than markets. Scholte similarly calls for a reformist globalization which advances human security, social equality and democracy.[7]

Such globalizations in the anglophone inter- and non-state Commonwealths have distinctive dimensions and inclinations, which contribute to global coalitions or campaigns like EITI and KP treated in the next chapter. Here I just highlight a couple of them—first, the nexus of migrations, diasporas and remittances, and second, small (island) states (SIDS)—which lead to contributions to global (and anti- or alter-globalization) as well as Commonwealth studies. Because the Commonwealths have come to involve continuing dialogues with global reach among diverse communities and sectors, especially inter- and non-state, they tend to moderate extremes, leading toward partnerships rather than polarization, as symbolized by their governance triangle as shown in Figure I.1.

Globalizations and the Commonwealths: how compatible?

Globalizations in the Commonwealth have, then, evolved in both state and non-state, civil society and private sector domains, posing implications for governance. Here I focus on migrations, diasporas and remittances and related "Commonwealth capitalisms"; i.e. distinctive patterns of non-Anglo-American capitalisms such as Indian or South African. These constitute distinctive Commonwealth variants of contemporary "varieties of capitalism" such as the Chinese, European, Japanese, etc., as well as the established transatlantic Anglo-American varieties.

First, though, there are significant numbers of professionals especially in educational—teachers and professors—and health—doctors and nurses—sectors from the Commonwealths working in countries other than those of origin, mainly in Britain and Canada but also in Botswana, South Africa, etc. So there are now more Malawian doctors in Manchester than back home in Malawi. In response to such global tensions, Commonwealth education ministers negotiated an understanding on teacher recruitment at their conference in Edinburgh at CCEM15, at the end of 2004. Such mobility now includes returnees such as Indian IT specialists going back to Bangalore for professional reasons or Caribbean migrants returning to their island of origin to retire. As Srinivasan recently suggested by contrast to more economistic formulations or definitions:

> Perhaps, in searching for a "Commonwealth factor," the greatest economic benefit in Commonwealth membership is to be found in the diaspora of various ethnic groups in the former Empire, and the British-oriented background of various professional classes like doctors, architects and engineers.[8]

Second, relatedly, in turn such professional mobility leads to substantial and rising remittance flows, especially from North to South, which surged at the dawn of the new millennium despite the momentary disruption but also potential longer-term retaliatory threats arising from 9/11. Despite such new security difficulties, by mid-decade this had become a global flow of at least $160 billion, which the IFIs only "discovered" belatedly, admitting that for some (35–40) developing economies—the more "fragile" states or economies—such remittances are already larger than either DFI or ODA. These flows are not exclusive to the Commonwealths, of course, though their encouragement or facilitation of migrations means a parallel generation and transmission of remittances.[9]

In its first-ever report on global remittances, the Bank recognized that the largest flows are to India, China, Mexico and the Philippines, with those to India rising especially rapidly at the turn of the century from $10 to $20 billion per annum up from just $5 billion in the mid-1990s.[10] Moreover, remittances make up a high proportion of GNP and the largest export income in small Commonwealth economies like Tonga, Lesotho, Jamaica and Samoa. A related DFID survey in the mid-2000s found that this flow was primarily to parents and other close relatives for food, health, and educational expenses in Commonwealth states—Nigeria, India, Pakistan, Jamaica and Ghana—which contributed to somewhat better HDI scores.

Such remittance flows, then, constitute a significant proportion of GNP and help to reduce poverty and advance MDGs in some Commonwealth and other countries. Northern donors like DFID, along with the banking industry, are now working to facilitate such transfers. The symbols or logos of these remittance flows—Western Union (250,000 agents globally) and Money Gram (100,000 agents)—are ubiquitous in the Commonwealth as well as elsewhere, especially in Mexico and the United States. For example, the former agency has 110 agents in Accra, 55 in Kampala and 15 in Kingston; the latter, 40 in Karachi, 100 in Kingston, 180 in Lagos and 150 in Mumbai with 150 in London, 125 in Birmingham and 95 in Manchester along with 160 in Toronto and 50 in Vancouver. And Money Mart's 1,000 outlets facilitate such Western Union and other remittance flows from Canada, the UK and the United States. Meanwhile, bi- and multilateral donors are developing ODA projects around remittances following major cosponsored conferences in London and elsewhere.

Finally, aside from radicalized youth, there is another dimension to such migration, diaspora and remittance nexuses, with their own security implications: "Commonwealth crime" networks. Gains from the erstwhile Commonwealth factor can be seized through informal and illegal economies as well as by the more familiar formal and legal ones. Such networks or mafias trade in drugs, guns, forced migration, money-laundering, the sex industry, etc. They include a wide variety of Commonwealth communities, with the Jamaicans and Nigerians being especially notorious in, say, Canada and South Africa, respectively, whether justifiably or not. Such networks can also support "global" terrorism, such as Canadian and other Tamils' support for the Tigers' struggle in Sri Lanka.

Such social changes impact micro- to macro-level globalizations. As is noted in the next chapter, Commonwealth corporations are increasingly active in global capital and technological sectors. And burgeoning Indian and South African capitalisms may have a somewhat different *modus operandi* from established Anglo-American varieties as in the ABC. So Tata Steel in competition with CVN from fellow BRIC, Brazil, competed to buy Corus in late 2006, thus joining Mittal as two of the top half-dozen global steel producers. Tata had already bought Tetley Tea and had developed Tata consulting into a major ICT player centered in Bangalore. It also has new major interests in steel in South Africa and instant coffee in Uganda. And South African corporations, even if legally or formally located in London, are major players in global beer, diamond, gold and related sectors, including services throughout Africa dependent on supply chain management, etc.—airlines, banking and insurance, grocery and clothing chains, shopping malls, etc.—such as familiar brands like De Beers, SABMiller (see Box 4.1 and Table 3.2).

Box 4.1 Commonwealth multinational corporations

Australia: Rupert Murdoch's News Corporation, the leading global media company with assets concentrated in Australia, Asia and Britain of some US$60 billion and annual revenues of over US$25 billion; major assets include Fox, Sky and Star television and satellite networks; Australian, Sun and Times newspapers; HarperCollins publishing, etc.; has transformed cricket, football and rugby globally (www.newscorp.com).

Australia: BHPBilliton is the world's largest diversified resources company based in Melbourne and London with assets of over US$120 billion and annual turnover of some US$40 billion; major player in copper, diamonds, energy, nickel, steel, etc., with operations in several Australian states, Southeast Asia (including Malaysia and Papua New Guinea), Canada, Chile, the UK and the United States (www.bhpbilliton.com).

India: The Tata Group is India's largest private sector conglomerate, with assets of over US$50 billion, active in myriad sectors, especially automobiles, chemicals, consumer products like coffee and tea, hotels, ICT, services and steel with a major commitment to Indian HE and R&D; it has many strategic alliances (e.g. with Sky TV and Tetley Tea), is growing in Africa with branches in many parts of Commonwealth Africa (especially Ghana, Mozambique, Nigeria, South Africa, Uganda, and Zambia) and sponsors brand ambassadors from India in cricket, racing cars, tennis, etc. (www.tata.com).

South Africa: Anglo American is one of the world's largest mining and industrial conglomerates with a turnover of some US$35 billion pa. It is the largest producer of platinum and a major producer of diamonds (De Beers), coal, gold (AngloGoldAshanti), metals, paper, tarmac, etc., with global operations concentrated in Australia, Botswana, Canada, the EU, Ghana, Namibia, Tanzania, etc. (www.angloamerican.co.uk).

South Africa: Stanbic is representative of South African companies' active interaction with the rest of the Commonwealth on the continent, from supermarkets and fast food to other service sectors and supply chains. It is South Africa's largest bank in the continent of Africa—R100 billion capitalization and R750 billion assets—with 230 branches with 380 ATMs in some 20 countries outside South Africa (compared to 750 branches and 3,800 ATMs inside the country). Its African branches are almost all within the Commonwealth: from Ghana and Nigeria to all of EAC and almost all of SADC, including Mauritius. Major shareholders include Old Mutual and Sanlam. Its representation outside the continent concentrates on the emerging economies or BRICs (www.stanbic.com).

Such changes reinforce the Commonwealths' roles in evolving global governance like the EITI and KP parallel to the UN Global Compact, as outlined in the next chapter. Before turning to global and Commonwealth studies, however, I highlight one area identified by Armstrong's opening citation, in which the Commonwealths have been consistently central by contrast to other regional and global agencies: SIDS.

Center for small states advocacy

Since their expansion in the Caribbean then Pacific oceans in the two or three decades following 1960, which coincided with global attention to the Law of the Sea deliberations and declarations, the Commonwealths have come to encourage attention to islands and oceans issues as unanticipated consequences of globalizations, arguably an area of their comparative advantage. As the Cold War ended, the secretary-general advanced recognition of global issues around human development and human security in small states. Given that some 32 of its 53 members are small, Paul Sutton suggests, "The Commonwealth has emerged as the intergovernmental champion for small states."[11] This recognition began in the early 1980s as many of the Caribbean island states joined small African (independence and membership in the 1960s) and Pacific (1970s then 1990s) members in achieving formal independence. But UN attention peaked around the Law of the Sea discussions and definitions in the early 1980s, then largely abandoning the issue-area to occasional global conferences like the decanal series on SIDS, functional agencies and other global organizations like ComSec.

McIntyre argues that "The Commonwealth has, indeed, become the premier small state forum."[12] As it expanded so its proportion of island and small states members increased (see Appendix 1), thus this became a natural role for it to assume. And if Overseas Territories (OTs) become formally associated with ComSec, as they have already with CGF and CPA, then its attention to small island states could grow even further. Sutton identifies a trio of small state-related areas in which it has become active:

> advocacy of their cause through development of the concept of vulnerability; policy advice in governance and economic development, with a focus on the joint study with the World Bank on the economic problems of small states; and the provision of technical assistance.[13]

In several reports from the mid-1980s onwards ComSec emphasized such members' "vulnerability": ecological, economic and social. As noted in the next paragraph, vulnerability has become something of a Commonwealth mantra, degrees of it being routinely assessed (e.g. see ComSec, Malta, Swiss, Diplofoundation *et al.*'s discussions in Malta on small state diplomacy in February 2007). In the early 1990s, around the Barbados Conference and subsequent Program of Action on Small Island Developing States (SIDS), Ministerial and Consultative Groups were established; these confirmed "the claim of the Commonwealth to speak with authority in the interests of small states."[14] And by the turn of the century, ComSec had come to do so in association with larger players like the World Bank: a continuing Joint Task Force to advance advocacy wing, policy advice, and technical assistance, including the Secretariat's annual economic review of SIDS.

The intergovernmental grouping of SIDS now numbers some 50 states—from small to mini- and micro-states—or a quarter of the global total. And its advocacy, the semi-state grouping of the Association of Small Island States (AOSIS) seeks to advance development interests through the identification of novel issues. Finally, a popular, non-state network which generates such issues is the global Internet forum of the Small Islands Voice.

ComSec undertook and advocated studies on "vulnerability," both geographical and globalization-related, from the mid-1980s onwards: *Vulnerability: small states in the global society*. Such vulnerability has evolved from geographical distance to sea-level rise, new security issues, natural disasters, migrations and diasporas, drugs and gangs and cruise ships. In particular, the Caribbean fought against demands to curtail "financial services", a.k.a. money-laundering, by allying with major financial actors. And SIDS increasingly advances novel forms of island and ocean governance. Further, association with or incorporation of the OTs would enhance its numerical membership even further. Sutton suggests that, in the post-bipolar era, given globalization, SIDS have more legitimacy and visibility than before via the Commonwealths, in part because they lack such a platform elsewhere in the contemporary global institutional architecture.[15]

The SIDS summit in Mauritius more than 10 years after the initial one in Barbados (April-May 1994) reflects such Commonwealth-centric preoccupations and prospects. It was intended to draw attention once again to such states' distinctive developmental difficulties, especially given exponential global warming and the ominous decline in fish stocks. As fate would have it, the United States and other powers conspired to have the Mauritius follow-up postponed from mid-1994 until January 2005. Thus it came to immediately follow rather than precede the December tsunami: this regional disaster throughout the Indian Ocean added urgency and poignancy to the proceedings.

Incidentally, it is not coincidental that two of the middle-income island states in the Commonwealth—Barbados then Mauritius, arguably both "developmental" as well as democratic states—came to host such global gatherings. By contrast to some island states, they have the capacity and resources to do so. The next chapter treats the political economy of competing for and actually hosting such mega-events both inside and outside the Commonwealths. Indeed, the Commonwealths may come to suggest or highlight another variety of developmental state: that of island developmental states like Barbados and Mauritius, emulating the examples of the quintessential SIDS—Singapore—along with Trinidad and Tobago and the OT of Bermuda (see Tables 4.1 and 4.2).

Tony Payne has juxtaposed his concentration on environment, finance and trade as development issues—the trio of arenas on which he focuses in his latest book on *The Global Politics of Unequal Development*—with the claims of small states, suggesting, in contrast to Sutton, that collectively they have been rather unsuccessful in

Table 4.1 Types of Commonwealth states and economies

OECD	Australia, Britain, Canada, New Zealand
BRIC	India
IBSA	India, South Africa
NIC	Singapore, Malaysia
Developmental state	Botswana, Brunei, Mauritius, Trinidad and Tobago
SIDS	Antigua, Bahamas, Cyprus, Dominica, Fiji, Grenada, Jamaica, Kiribati, Maldives, Malta, Nauru, Papua New Guinea, Samoa, Solomon Islands, St Kitts-Nevis, St. Lucia, St. Vincent, Tonga, Vanuatu
LDC	Bangladesh, Belize, Cameroon, Gambia, Ghana, Guyana, Kenya, Lesotho, Malawi, Mozambique, Nigeria, Seychelles, Sierra Leone, Swaziland, Tanzania, Uganda, Zambia
Fragile state	Cameroon, Dominica, Fiji, Gambia, Guyana, Kenya, Kiribati, Nigeria, Papua New Guinea, Sierra Leone, Solomon Islands, Tonga, Vanuatu

attracting resources in response to their particular needs: "Small states are mostly acted upon by much more powerful states and institutions. ... Vulnerabilities rather than opportunities ... come through as the most striking manifestations of the consequences of smallness in global politics."[16] Payne has also made major contributions to the parallel discourses on development, Commonwealth and global studies, to which I now turn following the above on small states and the non- as well as inter-state Commonwealths.

Commonwealth and/or global studies?

Unfortunately, Commonwealth studies—analyses of and debates around Commonwealth communities, communication, conflicts, cultures, ecologies, economics, education, health, histories, literatures, politics, sociologies, sports, etc.—tend to be overlooked in seemingly proximate analytic fields like comparative politics and international relations along with increasingly well established development studies and now global or globalization studies plus "new" security studies. Given their foci, as indicated by this book's table of contents, they should have long ago been recognized as relevant to overlapping area, comparative, development and regional studies, if not initially global or security studies. Such cosmopolitan Commonwealth studies in the twenty-first century can span local to global levels of analysis with a focus on national and international case studies concentrated but not exclusively so in the Commonwealths' extended family of inter- and non-state institutions.

As the Symons Commission on Commonwealth Studies suggested a decade ago:

> Commonwealth studies, though clearly overlapping at some points with area and regional studies, by their nature often involve a wider trans-regional ... perspective. ... Similarly, Commonwealth studies will often overlap development studies.[17]

The Symons Commission noted that the "cultural Commonwealth" builds on a broad common heritage, across South-North, small-large divides, of cultures, institutions, values and languages, with the latter working language happening to have become the lingua franca of globalization. But the Commission also urged the field to come up to date for applied as well as academic reasons:

> Commonwealth countries have ... focused on tomorrow's challenges of new information technology, of environmental protection, of controlling money laundering and commercial crime, of plural societies, and of the participation of NGOs in development, for example.
>
> This emphasis on the contemporary and the future is in contrast to a preoccupation with the past, and to a dwelling on the imperial, independence and post-independence phases of the Commonwealth's evolution.[18]

Clearly, Commonwealth studies can learn from and contribute to comparative studies of the majority of non-Commonwealth states and regions, especially between anglophone and other Commonwealths as identified in Chapter 1. But they can also go beyond the formal intra-Commonwealth to analyze informal, somewhat extra-Commonwealth, relations, such as those of the Commonwealths' diasporas and the flow of remittances to countries and communities of origin, as indicated above. Commonwealth cultural, educational, literature, sports and social ties bring the more formal and informal together, especially through contemporary ICTs like mobile phones and the Internet, including text messaging. And, as I suggest in the concluding pair of chapters, the Commonwealths may have a distinct advantage in riding the wave of globalizations because of their anglophone heritage, particularly of language and culture but also of mobility and flexibility.

As Tony Payne suggested himself at the turn of the century, informed by crafting the very helpful report which led in the first half of the first decade of the new millennium to the revival and redirection of the Institute of Commonwealth Studies in the University of London with which he was associated, while Commonwealth studies will always be a minor field,

> there can still be discerned a core of Commonwealth Studies which constitutes a coherent intellectual agenda for this field of study at the beginning of a new century. It should be built, in my view, around four disciplines ... in as integrated a fashion as possible.[19]

The four overlapping fields which Payne proceeded to identify were history, "the founding discipline," international relations, comparative politics and political economy. He also recognized that related genres like Commonwealth literature and other social sciences such as development studies and new security studies could also contribute. He concluded, perhaps somewhat optimistically, that, "the four highlighted disciplines—if pursued *in combination* and *in appropriate dialogue*—stand the best chance of giving Commonwealth Studies a new and interesting lease of life at the beginning of the twenty-first century."[20]

As already noted in the previous section, Payne subsequently reinforced his claims for the continued relevance of Commonwealth studies by reference to the distinctive place of small states in the global politics of development, recognizing that such states have more salience and status in inter- and non-state Commonwealths than most other global forums. By reference to the trio—environment, finance and trade—of major global arenas, "He concludes that small states have been largely unsuccessful in asserting their own interests in global politics, and that ... vulnerabilities rather than opportunities are the most striking consequence of smallness in global politics."[21]

In his major book on the structural inequalities to which development (as ideology as well as policy, practice and theory) is a response, Payne argues that innovative diplomacy by emerging economies and others (I would advocate the inclusion of "emerging" Southern civil societies and multinational companies as burgeoning sources for such public diplomacy) can transcend inherited inequalities. New drivers on novel issues can advance innovative forms of multilateralism (e.g. in response to new security threats, ecological challenges, multi-cultural tensions, etc.):

> Such gains as will be made over the next period of years in the direction of more equal development will be made by disadvantaged countries, operating mostly in shifting alliances, forcing concessions

and changes of current policy in finance or trade or the environ-ment by harnessing and deploying effectively the resources of power, however limited, that they do have at their disposal.[22]

However, as anticipated in the opening chapter, these interrelated Commonwealth, small state and development studies may now be increasingly threatened by emerging global or globalization studies. In the new millennium, scholars of world affairs are beginning to draw a distinction between international relations and global politics, with the latter being suggestive of a more comprehensive, structural integration however unequal: "the greater intensity and complexity of the con-nections that bind states, societies and other institutions in the present era."[23] I conclude this chapter by noting the place of the Common-wealths in pro- and anti-globalization discourses, before turning in Chapter 5 to the emergence and identification of particular Common-wealth niches.

Pro- and anti-globalization and global studies

Globalizations, plural—cultures and ideologies as well as institutions and interactions—seek to capture the essence of the compression of time and space; novel production, distribution and consumption "value chains"; and innovative governance structures of networks and part-nerships rather than government *per se* … as well as related inequal-ities. As with contemporary development, global fissures are no longer only North-South, East-West large-small or even urban-rural but rather multiple, now exacerbated by the emerging economies of the BRICs, especially China and India. The latter not only challenge established industries and entrepreneurs in the North, they increasingly impact resource-producing countries/regions in the South, especially Africa.[24] This has begun to lead to the notion of a post-bipolar "three worlds" which James Wolfensohn outlined in his 2006 Commonwealth Lec-ture: first, the OECD; second, the BRICs and the NICs; then third, the rest, especially fragile states (see Tables 4.1 and 4.2). Meanwhile, the range of global issues multiplies into biodiversity, certification and regulation, child workers and child soldiers, drugs, energy, guns, HIV/ AIDS and other viruses, migrations and diasporas, etc.

Anti- or alter-globalization advocacy in the Commonwealths—e.g. Martin Khor comes from Malaysia, Naomi Klein is Canadian (see her iconic *No Logo*)[25] and Vandana Shiva is Indian—is in part a reflection of activism through their burgeoning civil societies. So one can ask, along with David McIntyre, how compatible are such NGOs and

Table 4.2 World Bank typology of economies in Commonwealth per capita

High income *(US$10,726 and above)*	Antigua and Barbuda, Australia*, Bahamas, Brunei, Canada*, Cyprus, Malta, New Zealand*, Singapore, UK* (NB also Bermuda and Caymans as OTs plus Channel Islands and Isle of Man) (10)
Upper-middle income *($3,466–10,725)*	Barbados, Belize, Botswana, Dominica, Grenada, Malaysia, Mauritius, Seychelles, South Africa, St. Kitts-Nevis, St. Lucia, St. Vincent and the Grenadines, Trinidad and Tobago (13)
Lower-middle income *($876–3,465)*	Cameroon, Fiji, Guyana, Jamaica, Kiribati, Lesotho, Maldives, Namibia, Samoa, Sri Lanka, Swaziland, Tonga, Vanuata (13)
Low income *(less than $875)*	Bangladesh, Gambia, Ghana, India, Kenya, Malawi, Mozambique, Nigeria, Pakistan, PNG, Sierra Leone, Solomon Islands, Tanzania, Uganda, Zambia (15)

Notes:
Richest in Commonwealth: UK ($35,485 p.a.);
poorest in Commonwealth: Malawi ($149 p.a.).
* OECD member states

think tanks with the several capitalisms in Commonwealth?[26] In the triangle of tri-sector relations in the Commonwealths (see Figure I.1), how compatible is Commonwealth capitalism with civil society? Is the horizontal axis one of civil society-private sector coexistence and collaboration or opposition and antagonism? Similar questions can be posed to the UN Global Compact.[27]

In response to such debates, as indicated in the Introduction above, global and/or globalization studies are beginning to proliferate, including renewed attention to myriad security issues. These in part are beginning to augment or compete with increasingly established development studies, especially in the United States, where the latter have never become established or recognized. Thus, Commonwealth studies may yet contribute to global studies even if neither side so appreciates or even welcomes it thus far.

I turn in the two final chapters to some of the reasons for attention to overlapping Commonwealth, development and global studies: global competition and the future of the Commonwealths.

5 Commonwealths and the competition
What niches?

> ... the Commonwealth can be seen as having provided one international forum for the gradual emergence of a consensus around values of good governance, human rights and democracy.
>
> (Vicky Randall)[1]

As already indicated, following the Commonwealths' helpful contribution to global decolonization in general and invaluable role in ending apartheid in Southern Africa in particular, by the last decade of the twentieth century there was apprehension that its shelf-life had become limited. However, despite the momentary euphoria of the end of bipolarity, around the start of the new century the Commonwealths' utility now seems set for some time to come as it extends its reach toward advancing human security as well as human development and human rights. Arguably, this implies going beyond familiar sectors like democratic governance and small island states into new relatively unfamiliar and uncharted territory such as inter-racial communication and the management of globalization. Clearly, this entails an element of risk, but a limited and worthwhile one given the debilitating, corrosive effects of 7/7 along with 9/11.

This chapter suggests that the Commonwealths may have emerged from being the core of an epistemic community in the 1970s and 1980s, as we saw in Chapter 2, to aspiring to become a center for new multilateralisms in the new century; i.e. non- as well as inter-state coalitions. It identifies and analyzes partnerships around distinctive CGF and CBC over (athletic and economic, respectively) competitiveness, along with Commonwealth Plus coalitions around more the familiar Extractive Industries Transparency Initiative (EITI) and Kimberley Process (KP) for human development and human security. In so doing it adopts and extends the Commonwealth "governance" triangle of state/non-state relations presented in Chapter 1. Given the range of unanticipated Commonwealths' initiatives in the twenty-first century, it is apparent that they have become more than a sum of their parts.

My thesis is that the Commonwealths are more influential than just ComSec and inter-state memberships alone because global anglophone civil societies and multinational companies are dominant in sectors like democratic and sustainable development and in mining and telecommunications, respectively. Such status reflects the place of leading NGOs in Bangladesh, India and South Africa as well as in the Philippines, and of major MNCs in India and South Africa as well as in Brazil and China (the emerging economies or BRICs or BRICSA depending on selection of eligible countries). The Commonwealths are, then, reflections of members' communities and companies, not just states, who are represented through the Secretariat.

So, arguably, the Commonwealths punch above their weight in a series of interrelated sectors—culture including sports, education, economics, health, technology, etc.—given the inherited and inherent advantage of anglophone networks. These derive from the imperial legacy of investments in mining as well as colonial primary commodities like coffee, cotton and tea. In turn, at times encouraged by ABC, the Commonwealths have been in the avant-garde around corporate codes of conduct—agreed certification and regulation regimes—arising from tri-sectoral discussions and negotiations.

In future, such rules and norms should begin to be applied to civil societies and national regimes as well as international companies. For example, in mid-2006, a dozen, mainly larger transatlantic INGOs drafted and endorsed an INGO Accountability Charter. As something of an exemplar, in 2005 and 2006, the UK parliament's One World Trust has evaluated the compliance of a growing range of international organizations, INGOs and MNCs with accountability and transparency requirements: some 10 international organizations like the IBRD, ILO, IMF, WHO and WTO; another 10 MNCs from Anglo-American and Nestlé to News Corporation, Toyota and Wal-Mart; with the 10 INGOs including large ones like Amnesty, Oxfam, World Vision and WWF. The main findings from its "2006 Global Accountability Report" are available online; it will assess another 30 in 2007, revisiting the initial group in 2008. Also KP already has a monitoring system and EITI is establishing an international office in Norway to monitor compliance. The definition, implementation and evaluation of burgeoning corporate and sectoral codes has become something of a global growth industry, with a particular focus on consumer goods, extractive industries and service sectors.

Increasingly, then, like public agencies elsewhere at all levels, the Commonwealths' priorities are a function of the majority of their heterogeneous members; non- as well as inter-state. NGOs and MNCs along with think tanks are growing sources of policy initiatives such as Publish What You Pay over oil and mineral revenues and Partnership Africa Canada over conflict diamonds. Commonwealth Plus suggests the potential for leverage via strategic alliances with compatible networks around as well as inside Commonwealth members: public diplomacy around strategic sectors for Commonwealth companies and countries.

In this penultimate chapter, I turn from educational to cultural Commonwealths, and then the emerging agenda around faiths and confidence-building, toward economic Commonwealths and the political economy of the Commonwealth Games and other global mega-events before turning to the conclusion. Such dynamism in a variety of sectors may be contrasted with the relative concentration of attention along with modesty of creativity apparent in the several non-anglophone Commonwealths identified in the first chapter.

Educational Commonwealths

The educational and cultural Commonwealths overlap, of course, especially around their common usage or privileging of English, now the lingua franca of globalization. David Crystal has argued that, "at present, English is the only language in a position to adopt the role of the world's first language ... due primarily to the economic superiority of the United States, there is no competitor."[2]

Because of the global role of this rather than other ex-imperial languages, English is increasingly the language of global corporations and global higher education, as well as of global civil society. Thus graduate programs throughout the new EU of 25 or 27 members are increasingly in English, and English language texts sell in their millions in China as well as in India, Japan as well as Jamaica. As David Graddol notes in a recent report for the British Council, the reason for "the current enthusiasm for English in the world is closely tied to the complex processes of globalization ... the future of English has become more closely tied to the future of globalization itself."[3]

So the Commonwealths play a larger role in global education than just ACU, CSC and COL as Australia, Britain, Canada, India, New Zealand and South Africa become recognized as major players because of their mix of world-class universities and global publishing houses. This extends into flexible distance learning for educational and cultural industries exploiting burgeoning telecommunications networks.

Cultural Commonwealths

The turn of the century has witnessed the growth of the "cultural" Commonwealths, as in the scale of the Commonwealth Games as a set of global events now including extensive arts programming. Commonwealth cultural networks increasingly embrace "Commonwealth literature," including the annual Writers' Prize, plus Commonwealths' film and music. These cannot be separated from the economic or corporate nexus given growing private sector roles in cultural industries globally, from publishers to film studios, media celebrities to the Internet.

After Hollywood, the largest film/video industries in the world are now found in the Commonwealths: India (Mumbai) and Nigeria (Lagos)—Bollywood and Nollywood, respectively. In turn both of these are encouraged by demand in their respective diasporas, especially in the UK and US. But South Africa's continental DSTv satellite system now broadcasts Nollywood episodes 24/7 on its African Magic station. And it is no coincidence that some of the major global newspaper (and now multimedia) empires are located in the Commonwealths as well as the United States, and not just Britain, as is apparent in the case of Rupert Murdoch's global media empire based in his native Australia: News Corporation. But alternative, often anti-globalization, media such as Indymedia and Adbusters are also largely anglophone.

One distinctive, "informal" yet enduring Commonwealth connection arises from youth mobility: the established rite of passage of young Australians, Canadians, New Zealanders and South Africans trekking to London for a few months or years before settling down to middle-aged, middle-class professional life back home. Likewise, youthful Brits flock to the Antipodes if not yet to Canada, although Antipodeans cross the Pacific and equator to it, now increasingly part of a Pacific Rim phenomenon. As one minor dimension of globalizations, facilitated by inexpensive air travel, backpacking has become a distinct segment of global tourism, especially in anglophone Commonwealth countries like India, Malaysia and Singapore as well as Britain. In turn, it has spawned related sectors like the popular anglophone travel guides, increasingly available online.

I now turn to global anglophone civil society networks which are also often Commonwealth Plus in character and composition, constituting some of the distinctive context for the Commonwealths' inter- and nongovernmental relations and directions.

Commonwealths of civil societies

Given the heuristic qualities of the Commonwealth governance triangle introduced in Chapter 1, I broaden my ambit here from established Commonwealth Foundation and professional associations to a Commonwealth "Plus" spectrum of Commonwealth-centric INGOs such as Oxfam and VSO but also, say, AKF which operates primarily in Commonwealth Eastern Africa, South Asia, Canada and the UK (see Appendix 3).

As indicated in the previous chapter, some of largest INGOs are to be found in the Commonwealths in part because of their history of democracy and in part because of their language of operation; e.g. BRAC and Grameen in Bangladesh, plus AKF, Amnesty International, Oxfam or VSO in the UK and elsewhere. Some also have headquarters outside the Commonwealth family, such as in the United States—for example, CARE, PLAN International or World Vision—even if many of their operations are inside Commonwealth countries and communities.

Box 5.1 Commonwealth nongovernmental organizations

Bangladesh: the Bangladesh Rural Advancement Committee was founded in 1972 and now as Building Resources Across Communities (BRAC) operates in all 64 Districts of Bangladesh, with 4.8 million members in 65,000 villages. It is 75 percent self-funded via micro-credit bank, dairy and food projects (1998 onwards) and retail handicraft stores called "Arang." BRAC has gradually diversified into rural development programs over the last two decades, including primary health (1979) and solar energy (1997).

From 1975 it has undertaken development research through its Research and Evaluation Division (www.bracresearch.org). In 2001 it established a university to train development leaders, primarily in applied disciplines; it held its first graduation in January 2006 (www.bracuniversity.ac.bd). And in the new century BRAC International has begun to operate in Afghanistan, Sri Lanka (after the 2004 tsunami) and East Africa (Tanzania and Uganda and onto Southern Sudan) (www.brac.net).

Bangladesh: the Grameen Bank, which focuses on micro-credit for women from the poorest households in Bangladesh, was founded by an economics professor at Chittagong University, Muhammad Yunus, in 1976. It received the Nobel prize in 2006. Since 1983 the bank has made over 16 million loans of around US$100 each (94 percent to women), 98 percent of which have been repaid. By mid-decade it was lending US$600 million per annum to some 6 million members in 60,000 villages via 1,700 branches with 16,000 staff (www.grameen-info.org).

The Grameen family of some two dozen organizations now includes the Grameen Trust to replicate the bank globally, Grameen Fisheries, Grameen Knitwear and Grameen Communications (IT development)/ Telecom (mobile phones in village centers)/Cybernet (national Internet provider). Grameen is supported by bi- and multilateral donors like the EU, IBRD and UN plus US foundations like Clinton, Ford, MacArthur and Rockefeller. It also undertakes research via SIDE: Studies-Innovation-Development-Experimentation. Muhammad Yunus delivered the Commonwealth Lecture in London in March 2003.

United Kingdom: Oxfam is a global confederation of 13 national Oxfams, 5 of whom are Commonwealth, who operate in 11 regions, 5–6 of which are mainly Commonwealth with over 3,000 partners and a global expenditure of over US$525 annually. It started during World War II as the Oxford Committee for Famine Relief, and now engages in advocacy campaigns (offices in Washington D.C., New York, Brussels and Geneva), development education and programs, emergency relief, etc. Oxfam is part of the anti-corruption Publish What You Pay coalition behind EITI, and a founding signatory to the 2006 INGO Accountability Charter (www.oxfam.org).

United Kingdom: Voluntary Service Overseas (VSO) was an early British post-colonial NGO which grew out of the volunteering movement around young people in the late 1950s. It has supported over 30,000 volunteers in over 70 countries since then, now sending 2,000 each year to some 40 states, over half of which are Commonwealth members. It has since become more transnational, recruiting through offices in Commonwealth Canada, India, Kenya, and Uganda as well as non-Commonwealth Ireland, Netherlands, and the Philippines. It continues to develop a range of new programs (e.g. returned volunteers and tours to raise consciousness and finance) and alliances (e.g. with diasporas and businesses) to advance development education globally (www.vso.org.uk).

Furthermore, albeit somewhat more speculatively, I would also hazard that Commonwealth networks of development and other think tanks, such as ODI in London and NSI in Ottawa, impact Commonwealth and Commonwealth Plus deliberations and directions, both national and global, as indicated by the lists of eminent persons on the latest Expert Groups and Commissions (see Box 5.2). There is also a promising legacy of institutes of international relations established throughout the Dominions: from RIIA in London (now rebranded Chatham House) to Australian, Canadian, Indian, New Zealand and South African associates or parallels (including the University of West Indies (UWI)-based Institute of International Relations (IIR)). Given some similarities in approach, training and networks, these might become the centerpieces of a "Commonwealth school of international relations" to supersede or spread the erstwhile "English school" as suggested at the end of the following conclusion.

Relatedly, the generic international community has generated a set of innovative ideas and concepts through a series of global commissions over the last quarter-century, some of which became symbolic of contemporary issues; e.g. the Brandt, Brundtland and Palme reports. These have produced a set of timely responses to global debates from bipolar conflict to global governance, international development to humanitarian intervention, dams to health. The Commonwealth has generated its own series of Expert Group reports, particularly in the Ramphal era when it was closest to the ideology and diplomacy of the UN/Non-aligned systems: 10 between 1977 and 1987 (see Box 3.1). The only Commonwealth report to approach an iconic status comparable to that of the Brandt, Brundtland or Palme was that of a collectivity: the mid-1980s Eminent Persons Group on the apartheid regime: *Mission to South Africa*. The legacy of such innovative postwar UN-related multilateralist thinking is reflected in Weiss *et al.*'s *UN Voices*.[4] And ComSec is expecting equally authoritative policy directions or steers to emerge from the 2007 Amartya Sen Commission on respect and understanding.

Thus, global civil society can serve to bring overlooked issues into the global spotlight. Hence reluctant attention to, say, indigenous communities or small island states, is sometimes advanced by unanticipated crises like the December 2004 tsunami in the case of the latter. But how efficacious are the Commonwealths compared to, say, EITI or the Kimberley Process: how to create momentum through global coalitions of mixed actors?

Such skepticism becomes even more relevant as I now turn from the Commonwealths' governance triangle for human development to task expansion beyond human rights and on toward human security. This evolution reflects the multiplication of new security issues and increasingly apparent limits to so-called wars on terrorism.

Responding to global tensions: respect and understanding

The late-2001 CHOGM scheduled for Brisbane was postponed because of 9/11 and then the 7/7 "home-grown" bombs in London in mid-2005 disrupted the G8 summit in Scotland. But other Commonwealth countries were not immune, as was apparent in pre-9/11 terrorist attacks in Kenya and Tanzania. In response to global terrorisms and tensions, the Malta CHOGM and CPF for the first time directly addressed issues of religions and diversity. The latter held a day-long reflection on faith-based organizations and implications for the Foundation's programming. And the former's Communiqué from Valetta presented in Appendix 4 below called on ComSec "to explore initiatives to promote mutual understanding and respect among all faiths and communities in the Commonwealth." Both groupings are to report back to CHOGM/CPF in Kampala in late 2007 following consultations.

The ability of the Commonwealths' extended family to so consider is a tribute to its history and diversity. But all involved recognize that this is not only novel but also rather problematic and high-risk policy terrain, involving more risks than some other areas of public policy. To be sure, the British empire also involved religious dimensions, including varieties of Christian missionaries. And as Indian and other communities were encouraged to migrate within the empire, so religions like Hinduism and Sikhism spread to the Caribbean and Pacific islands as well as regions of Africa, eventually appearing, at least initially indirectly, in Canada and the UK. One of the unanticipated ironies of such history is the present split in the traditionally conservative global Anglican communion between inclusive, "liberal" Northern parishes and anti-homosexual Southern bishops and congregations, culminating in a very difficult church summit in Dar es Salaam in early 2007.

In late 2006, then, ComSec began to contemplate ways to frame its "respect and understanding" mandate and the Foundation advanced its parallel "faith and development" programming, informed by a multi-faith advisory group. But how can the Commonwealths together add value to others' established deliberations? The former constitutes something of an extension of its continuing good offices, governance prerogative; the latter, a correlate of its civil society and good governance purview. These parallel initiatives are intended to advance the Commonwealths' comparative advantage in such areas, to build on and extend Commonwealth values into arenas of social and religious conflicts and responsive confidence- and peace-building. The Commonwealth Commission on respect and understanding includes some of the world's leading thinkers and advocates (as indicated in Box 5.2). This is symptomatic of the Commonwealths' ability to attract as Commonwealth lecturers at century's turn such global figures as Kofi Annan (2000), Mary Robinson (2002), Muhammad Yunus (2003), and John Wolfensohn (2006).

Box 5.2 Memberships of latest Commonwealth expert groups/commissions, 2002–7

Manmohan Singh Expert Group on Development and Democracy 2002–3

- Manmohan Singh (India) (Chair) Leader of the Opposition in national parliament; Prime Minister 2004–
- Jocelyne Bourgon (Canada) Head of the Public Service (1994–99) then Ambassador to the OECD in Paris
- Robert Champion de Crespigny (Australia) leading entrepreneur who was Chair of the Economic Development Board of South Australia
- Richard Jolly (UK) previously Director of IDS at the University of Sussex followed by senior roles in UNICEF and UNDP
- Martin Khor (Malaysia) Director, Third World Network
- Akinjide Osuntokun (Nigeria) previously Ambassador to Germany and Professor of History at the University of Lagos
- Salim Ahmed Salim (Tanzania) previously Prime Minister, Secretary-General of the OAU and Ambassador to the UN
- Tuiloma Neroni Slade (Samoa) Judge at the ICC in The Hague; previously Ambassador to the UN
- Dwight Venner (St. Lucia) Governor of the Eastern Caribbean Central Bank
- Ngaire Woods (New Zealand) Director of the Global Economic Governance Programme at Oxford University; previously Rhodes Scholar (Commonwealth Secretariat 2003: 105–7)

**Amartya Sen Commission on Respect and
Understanding, 2006–7**

- Amartya Sen (India) Nobel Laureate, Oxford and Harvard
  Universities
- John Alderdice (UK) House of Lords and facilitator, Northern
  Ireland Peace Process
- Adrienne Clarkson (Canada) previously Governor-General and
  senior media personality
- Noeleen Heyzer (Singapore) Director of UNIFEM, New York
- Kamal Hossain (Bangladesh) previously Minister of Foreign
  Affairs
- Elaine Howard (Tonga) South Pacific Representative on
  Commonwealth Youth Caucus
- Wangari Mathai (Kenya) Nobel Laureate and leader of the
  Greenbelt Movement
- Rex Nettleford (Jamaica) previously Vice-Chancellor, University
  of the West Indies
- Mamphele Ramphele (South Africa) previously Vice-Chancellor,
  University of Cape Town and Managing Director, World Bank
- Lucy Turnbull (Australia) previously Lord Mayor of the City of
  Sydney

Both agencies and networks are beginning to seek to identify causes
and consequences of the alienation understood to lead toward fundamentalisms and terrorisms, along with subsequent levers for positive
change to be able to report to the next CHOGM/CPF in Kampala in
late 2007: lessons from and for Commonwealth states and societies.
Such insights would hold relevance for both national and regional
actors both inside and outside the Commonwealths.

The Secretariat's ten-person Commission on Respect and Understanding—the first ever with a female majority—reflects the best of
the Commonwealths: accomplished, cosmopolitan personalities and
thinkers (as indicated in Box 5.2). It is being chaired by Indian Nobel
laureate Amartya Sen, who previously co-chaired the UN's Commission
on Human Security, and includes eminent global and Commonwealth
citizens like Adrienne Clarkson (Canada), Noeleen Heyzer (Singapore),
Wangari Maathai (Kenya), Rex Nettleford (Caribbean) and Mamphele Ramphele (South Africa). It started its deliberations in December 2006 and is to report to the late-2007 Uganda summit on how
Commonwealth communities could and should bridge multiple divides

peacefully. "Respecting Difference and Promoting Understanding" was the theme for Commonwealth Day in March 2007, which was celebrated in a major way in Kampala as well as London ahead of the mid-November CHOGM. And the theme for the Kampala summit itself is "Transforming Commonwealth Societies to Achieve Political, Economic and Human Development."

I turn next to the economic dimensions of the Commonwealths; both their broader political economies and then their own specific mega-events which create special opportunities and entail certain risks, such as the relatively familiar biennial CHOGMs and quadrennial Commonwealth Games.

Economic Commonwealths

In addition to civil society and cultural networks, the economic or "corporate" Commonwealths give the nexus an influence larger than limited and uneven inter-state membership alone because so many of their economic and related institutions have relations throughout the Commonwealth and beyond, i.e. they overlap with other extra-Commonwealth networks. Such a perspective in this part constitutes a somewhat speculative extension of the Commonwealths beyond inter- and non-state agencies. This may be controversial in analytic and applied terms but does serve to reinforce the claim of the Commonwealths' nexus to more serious attention in relation to contributions to global governance in the complex and fraught contemporary period.

Just as in inter-state politics and non-state civil societies—two of the Commonwealths' three "triangular" sides—so in private economic sectors, the Commonwealths have a distinctive niche because of their imperial inheritance. This lies primarily in their educational, professional and technological institutions, along with an inherited emphasis on the energy and mineral sectors. Given the patterns of contemporary globalizations, which are primarily anglophone, "what Ford and Katwala refer to as the 'Commonwealth factor' in trade or 'common business culture' ... means that ... it is around 10–15 per cent cheaper to do business in another Commonwealth country than outside it."[5]

In terms of value in global supply chains in the contemporary global economy, colonial primary commodities are now less significant than post-colonial minerals, energy and communications plus the high-tech revolution, all facilitated by professional migration. Centerpieces of the world economy at the start of the twenty-first century include energy and minerals, given the booming demand from the BRICs, especially China and India, and ICTs from RIM in Ontario,

Canada to Tata in Bangalore, India. Nevertheless, the post-imperial core of mining as well as energy is still centered in Australia, Britain, Canada and South Africa as well as the two old superpowers of Russia and the United States. So some Commonwealth governments and companies are increasingly significant players in the contemporary global political economy, with implications for their relations with civil society including labor and consumers.

Because of the economic interests of the British empire, including its Dominions of white settlement, the established, industrialized powers in today's Commonwealth have significant mining infrastructures and investments at home and abroad. So, aside from Russia and the United States, the leading mineral states are Australia (e.g. BHP), Canada (e.g. Alcan) and South Africa (e.g. AngloAmericanAshanti), with London as the dominant center for such multinational investment (e.g. De Beers) (see Table 3.2 for an overview of the corporate Commonwealth).

The coincidence of major mining conglomerates and leading advocacy NGOs and think tanks in the Commonwealths, particularly the ABC and RSA, and especially London, has led to the emergence of a Commonwealth-centric version of the UN Global Compact: the Extractive Industries Transparency Initiative (EITI). The former Compact includes an extensive, heterogeneous range of members such as business schools, NGOs and universities. The latter Commonwealth-based energy and mining members include companies from Australia (e.g. BHP), Canada (e.g. Barrick, Talisman and Petro-Canada), India (e.g. several parts of the Tata conglomerate), South Africa (e.g. AngloGoldAshanti and Gold Fields), UK (e.g. BP, De Beers, Rio Tinto, SABMiller and Shell) (see Box 4.1).

EITI emerged in the second half of the 1990s from the stand-off between mining companies, Third World regimes and global civil society over corruption: the corrosive effects of MNCs buying favors in the South to facilitate the flow of energy and minerals. It also constituted something of a pre-emptive reaction to the burgeoning global coalition of some 300 NGOs concerned about informal or illegal corporate payments to governments to secure access to energy and mineral reserves: the Publish What You Pay campaign. This was founded in the UK by a set of largely compatible NGOs: CAFOD, Global Witness, Oxfam, Save the Children UK, Transparency International UK and others, encouraged by George Soros and the Open Society Institute. But it now has the support of 300 NGOs, forming coalitions in some 20 countries (over a dozen in the Commonwealth), including some oil, gas and mineral exporters (e.g. Australia, Botswana, Cameroon, Canada (10 NGOs), Ghana, Kenya, Mauritius, Nigeria (50 NGOs),

Pakistan, South Africa, Swaziland, Tanzania, UK (25 NGOs) and Zambia).

EITI seeks to ensure through good accounting and improved accountability that revenues from company payments to resource producers go to their citizens for their human development rather than to individuals in ruling regimes for personal or familial accumulation and aggrandizement. This reflects a growing World Bank, G8 and donor concern, although the NGO coalitions may adopt more direct, adversarial tactics in ensuring the publication of revenue streams.

EITI was advanced particularly by the Blair government in Britain in mid-decade and was endorsed by the Commission for Africa which met and reported ahead of the G8 summit at Gleneagles in mid-2006. Like the UN Global Compact, which companies as well as NGOs endorse so that they can wrap themselves in the blue UN flag, EITI has been supported, at least rhetorically, by leading Commonwealth mining and energy corporations, such as Anglo American, BP, BHP, Billiton, and De Beers.

A somewhat parallel though more specifically Commonwealth-centric initiative—a greater proportion of players is located and operates in Commonwealth states—at the turn of the century is the global campaign to ban blood diamonds, otherwise known as the Kimberley Process (KP). This seeks to cut-off the flow of informal and illegal diamonds produced by artisanal miners, which often leads to the importation of guns and other light weapons to secure the extractive sites and related supply chains. Because the threat of bad publicity would have undermined the established global industry, especially the De Beers monopoly, leading stakeholders agreed to adopt a form of preventative public diplomacy by gathering initially in the city in South Africa where the industry began: Kimberley. KP has been advanced by Commonwealth and other states affected—e.g. Australia, Botswana, Britain, Canada, India, Namibia, Sierra Leone, and South Africa—along with a range of NGOs, labor unions, cities (e.g. Kimberley and Mumbai) where mining and processing are concentrated, major diamond processors, and retailers. One of the leading players was a miniscule Canadian NGO: Partnership Africa Canada. The negative possibilities of such informal, illegal global supply chains anchored in Africa was graphically projected through the release of the movie *Blood Diamonds* in late 2006 and early 2007.

KP is now also leading to an effort to advance the sustainable development of the artisanal sector as well as the containment of informal, illegal production and distribution. The Diamond Development Initiative

(DDI) supported by the World Bank and bilateral donors, De Beers and other major stakeholders seeks to advance ecological, educational, labor, safety, social and technological relations which transcend the short-term calculus of current artisanal techniques. The diamond industry's experience with preventative public diplomacy constituted useful background in mid-decade when it confronted the negative PR fall-out from the above-mentioned major (South African-produced) movie *Blood Diamonds* starring Leonardo DiCaprio and Djimon Hounsou.

I now turn to the other major Commonwealth activity which has a significant financial component: the Games. Like the Olympics and other global sporting mega-events, like world cups for cricket, soccer or rugby, these now offer the opportunity for corporate sponsorship: a far cry from the economically as well as politically problematic era of sports boycotts and sanctions as core features of the anti-apartheid movement in the 1970s and 1980s.

Commonwealth Games: cultural as well as sports festival?

The four-yearly or quadrennial Games have become bigger global events than the biennial CHOGMs, even though, unlike the latter, almost all of them have been hosted in Australia, Britain, Canada and New Zealand, i.e. ABC. Like the latter, however, they have also become multi-media, multi-dimensional happenings, increasingly cosponsored by major Commonwealth and other corporations. Thus the 2002 Manchester and 2006 Melbourne Games attracted over 70 teams (including some from dependent overseas territories like Gibraltar) and coincided with large-scale cultural festivals and other tie-ins such as the Commonwealth Writers' Prize. For a dozen such Games, they have been preceded by a major conference on sports science in or around the host city: the Commonwealth International Sport Conference.

The next Games are scheduled for India in 2010, the focus of the closing ceremonies at Melbourne. Interestingly in terms of the emergence of the BRICs, especially China and India, the next summer Olympics are in Beijing in mid-2008. (NB The next winter Olympics are also in the Commonwealth: at Whistler, outside Vancouver, in British Columbia, Canada.) And, as indicated in the next section, Abuja, Glasgow and Halifax have been competing to host the following Commonwealth Games in 2014. As McIntyre suggests: "the Games are often the only point of popular identification with the Commonwealth for most of its peoples."[6]

Thus far in the twenty-first century, the Manchester and Melbourne Games of some score sports were matched by series of major cultural events: art, concerts, film, museum exhibits, music, street performances and theater let alone food and drink. The state of Victoria claimed that "Festival Melbourne 2006" was "Australia's biggest-ever festival of arts and culture." The preceding Thirteenth Commonwealth International Sport Conference in Melbourne, like its dozen predecessors, focused on sport coaching, sport science and medicine, sport management and sport studies. And the Commonwealth Foundation ensured that the annual Writers' Prizes coincided with the Festival and Games and that the winners were announced in Melbourne.

Major national and global corporate partners (mainly Commonwealth but also non-Commonwealth) for the 2006 Melbourne Games were National Australia Bank, Microsoft, Qantas, Tabcorp, Telstra, Toyota and Visa; 10 sponsors included Australia Post, Cadbury-Schweppes, De Bortoli Wines, Nestlé and PWC; and there were another dozen providers. Until such private support was available in the 1990s, the Games were financially very tenuous, financially as well as politically. And during the preceding era of anti-apartheid struggle in the 1970s and 1980s, they were boycotted by many teams from the South, especially Africa, rendering them even more economically as well as organizationally fragile and politically intense.

The Commonwealth Games of 21 sports includes a different selection of sports from the summer Olympics. For example, it features lawn bowls, netball, rugby, squash, etc. Such dimensions distinguish them from the more familiar, global Olympic mix of events. And several of these sports also feature as independent annual global competitions outside the quadrennial Games. Beijing 2008 will involve more countries and competitors than Delhi 2010.

Furthermore, Commonwealth Plus includes those distinctive international sports which are primarily but not exclusively located in Commonwealth countries and communities, for example bowls, cricket, field hockey, netball, and rugby. Some of these have also been transformed by interrelated changes in rules and media support, notably cricket and rugby. Here, the role of Australian media mogul Rupert Murdoch's Sky TV network, part of his News Corporation, has been central. Hence the ICC World Cup (South Africa 2003, West Indies 2007, South Asia 2011—i.e. amongst Commonwealth members) and Rugby World Cup (the majority being Commonwealth, but often including Argentina, France, Ireland, Japan and the US), and rugby's Six Nations Championship (Europe) and Tri-nations competition (among ex-Dominions in the southern hemisphere), etc.

I now conclude this chapter by examining the political economy of competitions to host such major Commonwealth events: a subset of the burgeoning events management discipline, literature and profession.

Hosting of Commonwealth events: costs and benefits

Any realistic global cost-benefit analysis of the Commonwealths for state and non-state members alike has now to include the economic and other gains as well as losses arising from hosting Commonwealth events, especially the larger more commercially exploitable ones like biennial CHOGMs and quadrennial Games. As the Commonwealths have become less British- or London-centric and as globalization facilitates the decentralization of communications and conferences, so major and minor cities have been able to bid for events like ministerial meetings, professional gatherings and corporate palavers. This is in addition to CHOGM, CPF and Commonwealth Games and their traditional related add-ons.

Aside from symbolism and visibility, the hosting of world events has become a major industry with its own analytic pedagogy, professional infrastructure and formal accreditation rules. And, unlike global institutions like the UN and IFIs, Olympics or world soccer, smaller states and cities can aspire to attract Commonwealth inter- or non-state happenings, including regional Commonwealth gatherings in, say, East, Southern or West Africa, the Caribbean or Pacific, even if the Games are beyond their imagination or reach.

Smaller states or cities can now invite ACU, CJA, CLA, CPA, etc., to hold conferences there. Thus, the first CHOGM outside London other than a prime ministerial meeting in Lagos in 1966 was Singapore in 1971. And island states like Jamaica (1975), Bahamas (Nassau) (1985), Cyprus (1993) and Malta (2005) have hosted the summit along with the widening set of parallel events around it, leading to Trinidad and Tobago in 2009, a developmental island state. CHOGMs have also been held in cities other than capitals (Melbourne 1981 and Brisbane 2001/2, Vancouver 1987, Auckland 1995, Edinburgh 1997 and Durban 1999). Barbados and Mauritius as island developmental states hosted the initial and follow-up SIDS jamborees of over 50 states along with inter- and nongovernmental organizations. And venues for the Commonwealth Games read like a tourist guide to global cities. Symbolically, the first major international event in Sierra Leone post-civil war was a pre-16CCEM (Cape Town, end-2006) regional Commonwealth Africa and Europe education ministers' review of open and distance education in Freetown in November 2005.

Cost-benefit analyses of global events remain controversial and Montreal is still paying for its Olympics of 1976. Some Commonwealth events, especially non-state, may be relatively inexpensive to host, but CHOGM, CPF and the Games constitute mega-investments and risks, as Brisbane discovered to its cost when 9/11 caused CHOGM to be postponed from late 2001 to early 2002, along with the separation of CPF which proceeded as planned. The Edinburgh CHOGM in 1997 was the largest international gathering in the UK since the first UN General Assembly in 1946 and Olympic Games in 1948, i.e. for half a century. Similarly, SIDS in Mauritius was postponed from late 2004 to early 2005, i.e. from before to after the Christmas 2004 tsunami. Recent Games in Manchester 2002 and Melbourne 2006 have been multi-media events involving a significant corporate presence with myriad cultural and educational dimensions, including the tradition of a major sports conference preceding the opening ceremonies. Thus Festival Melbourne 2006 was styled as the "biggest free cultural festival ever held in Australia" with a dazzling range of global to local exhibitions and performances at some core sites around the city.

Legacies of CHOGMs and Games include conference halls, sports stadia and swimming pools (e.g. Edmonton from 1978 and Victoria from 1994) as well as debts. But the invisible, perpetual gains of recognition and visibility are incalculable, such as the claim to Third World eminence of, say, art-deco Bandung in Indonesia which hosted the early generation of Afro-Asian nationalist leaders in 1955 and now sports a museum dedicated to its moment in the sun. Arguably, Hamilton, Ontario is still more famous for hosting the first Commonwealth Games in 1930 than for any subsequent role.

The Malta CHOGM/CPF/CBC in 2005, held as the two islands of Malta and Gozo joined the EU, constituted its largest-ever hosting. So intra- and extra-Commonwealth cosponsors of assorted activities included Air Malta, Bank of Valetta, BMW, GE and Maltacomgroup/gomobile. To mark the occasion and to advertise its capabilities, the island state had videos of the event playing on its national airline flying in and out of Valetta, and the national English press, the *Times of Malta* had daily supplements on CHOGM the week of the summit in late November.

Since securing the late-2007 CHOGM, Uganda has witnessed a building spree with new hotels, highways and malls being constructed or renovated in Kampala and Entebbe. Similarly, Trinidad already has a new international airport ahead of 2009 with an impressive waterfront of walkways and high-rise offices under construction. The management and orchestration, PR and logos, of CHOGMs and related meetings has become a minor industry, with planning starting ahead of the previous CHOGM. So Uganda was actively promoting its tourism attractions at Malta in late 2005.

Aside from the political economy of major international events, there is a burgeoning literature and practice of events planning and promotion. In the case of the Commonwealth, the major focus of attraction aside from the CHOGM syndrome is now the Games, which have taken on the professional aura of a mini-(summer) Olympics. Here, for illustration, I present a vignette of the bid by Halifax in Nova Scotia for the twentieth Games in 2014, until it withdrew its offer in early 2007, based on the calculation of costs rather than benefits. Its candidacy had been apparent from the international airport onwards—billboards, buses, newspaper ads featuring the bid—but it pulled its offer in early 2007 on grounds of being unable to support it financially as estimates had escalated.

Given contemporary bids and results, to secure the Canadian nomination then compete with Glasgow in Scotland and Abuja in Nigeria, Halifax had to assemble a compelling coalition of government, corporate, sports, media, communication, educational, tourism and other partners. The CGF is to announce the winner to follow the upcoming 2010 Games in New Delhi in November 2007 at its meeting in Sri Lanka just ahead of the Kampala CHOGM. The Halifax bid had the usual statement of vision and principles and had major support from three levels of government, the Bank of Nova Scotia and the leading regional supermarket chain, Sobeys, with other donors including the regional telecommunications (Aliant) and energy (Emera) corporations. Its bid emphasized competition, communications like a major airport, infrastructure, support, finance, environment, and on a scale such that many athletes would be able to walk to venues (the Commonwealth Games Village would have been in an ex-Canadian military facility, Shannon Park, close to the city center and major bridges and facilities). However, as with the 2012 London Olympics, costs for the Haligonian Games escalated to some C$2 billion, which none of the levels of government in Canada could afford, especially city and provincial. So in early 2007 Halifax dropped its bid, leaving 2014 down to a choice between Abuja and Glasgow.

The Halifax bid could claim to build on two distinctive strands: first, Canada's close association with the Games and second, Halifax's earlier global event: the G8 summit of 1995. First, the Games (of just eleven teams) started in Hamilton in 1930 and have returned to Canada every couple of decades: Vancouver in 1952 (22 teams),

Edmonton in 1978 (46) and Victoria in 1994 (63). Halifax would have expected some 70 teams at the twentieth Games, as several (roughly 20) non-independent countries regularly compete. And second, Halifax's other moment in the sun was June 1995 when it hosted the G8 summit and alternative civil society counter-conference. This pre-Seattle 1999 event was relatively low-key, endorsing the Highly Indebted Poor Country (HIPC) facility for the poorest states. The parallel NGO discussions led to the still-continuing Halifax Initiative, which encouraged the Jubilee 2000 debt relief campaign and related demands. But the G8 hosting was not the focus of a prior competitive bid as summits circulate among the eight member states, whose governments nominate a host location. And curiously, the G8 experience and expertise did not feature in the PR bid to the CGF in 2014, possibly an indication of the mixed message of being associated with a pro-globalization institution, at least in the twenty-first century, post-Seattle 1999.

Like biennial CHOGMs and now CPFs, most Commonwealth ministerial meetings hold to a regular pattern and the CBC cosponsors an endless series of major regional and sectoral activities. Ministerials include annual finance meetings, pre-IFI gatherings, foreign ministers' pre-UN General Assemblies each fall in New York, and pre-WHO health congresses in Geneva. Other conferences which occur regularly on two- or three-year cycles deal respectively with education, environment, gender, youth, and from March 2004, tourism.

This penultimate chapter has begun to identify niches for the contemporary Commonwealths and Commonwealth Plus. The final chapter looks at possible futures for both Commonwealths and the broader global communities. In so doing both have tried to begin to respond to the recent appeal by Vicky Randall, because as she says, timely analytic attention which looks "more directly and systematically at these questions about the character of the Commonwealth as community and organisation (as such) is long overdue."[7]

6   Commonwealths and the future

> The Commonwealth embarked on the new century nursing considerable satisfaction about the renaissance of the 1990s, while facing some urgent decisions about the association's future.
>
> (David McIntyre)[1]

The thesis of this conclusion is that the inter- and non-state Commonwealths will continue to have impact and respect, primarily because of their civil society, professional association and private corporate dimensions, even if they never approach the status or reach of the global UN or IFI institutions nor the regional EU or ASEAN organizations. And the NGO and MNC extensions of the Commonwealths are likely to grow in terms of numbers and issues faster than ComSec as they both respond to both demand and opportunity at the start of the twenty-first century, particularly in the anglophone worlds of communications, culture, ecology, economics, education, gender, health and technology: what I characterize as Commonwealth Plus. Moreover, in part because of its relative marginality, the intergovernmental Commonwealth, at least, post-apartheid, has never faced the crises which the UN confronted at the turn of the century around post-Cold War conflicts and internal accountability, legitimacy and transparency.

This conclusion progresses from a consideration of the Commonwealths in the context of uneven globalizations to their continuing institutional, applied and analytic contributions. It ends by proposing that such a juxtaposition may come to inform traditional international relations as well as constitute a positive response to the growing plea to learn from Africa about the salience of non-state cooperation and conflict.

Until the twenty-first century, what was good for GM was assumed to be good for the US. Now, what is good for much of civil society and private companies is good for the Commonwealths, given their close and growing associations with both such sectors, which are largely anglophone in character the world over. As already indicated, just as the Global Compact has extended the UN's reach, so the Commonwealth Business Council and Commonwealth Foundation have widened the Commonwealths' purview and increased their relevance. This is especially so as national as well as global MNCs develop in states like India and Singapore, and indigenous as well as international NGOs in members like Bangladesh and Kenya, as we saw in Chapters 3 and 5.

Commonwealths and globalizations

As the end of the first decade of the new century draws nearer, the resilience of the Commonwealths becomes more apparent in the face of myriad pressures, in part because they have never achieved the formalities of the IFI or UN systems or the complexities of the EU. As John Stremlau suggests:

> The Commonwealth thus faces a new strategic challenge: how to intervene effectively to help governments deal with increasing economic globalization amid demands for greater political self-determination. The Commonwealth's ... modest administrative structures ... and its rules of consensus are at once its greatest strength and weakness.[2]

Today's Commonwealths include states which rank highly on both "globalization" and "failed" (or fragile) states indices, both indicators of contemporary world politics as indicated in Table 4.1. Thus, on the one hand, the Commonwealths' high globalization states are, in order, Singapore, Canada, New Zealand, UK, Australia and Malaysia (in the *Foreign Policy* top 20). By contrast, on the other hand, their failed or fragile states consist of Pakistan, Sierra Leone, Bangladesh, Uganda, Nigeria and Sri Lanka (in the *Foreign Policy* bottom 25). To be sure, such rankings may be challenged on grounds of less-than-rigorous methods or data, yet they do present plausible ball-park listings. Hence the Commonwealths' relevance to the continuing, albeit changeable, North/South, rich/poor, central/marginal divides. But, if the official Commonwealth is but one amongst many global institutions, its unofficial dimensions are (or rather, should be) less readily overlooked or dismissed, despite the tendency of most of its analysts, even advocates, however positive, to so disregard.

As indicated in the previous chapter, the relative importance of the Commonwealths in "global" civil society is apparent by reference to some major Commonwealth-based or -centric INGOs; for example, AKF, Amnesty International, Oxfam and WWF in the UK; BRAC and Grameen in Bangladesh; Civicus and anti-HIV/AIDS TRAC in South Africa.

And likewise, Commonwealth MNCs which feature in Fortune 500 and related lists include AngloGoldAshanti, De Beers and SABMiller in South Africa; Birla, Indian Oil, Infosys, Reliance, State Bank and Tata in India; Flextronics in Singapore; Petronas in Malaysia; BHP Billiton, ANZ Banking and Telstra in Australia.

So, as already indicated in Chapter 5, both Commonwealth MNCs and NGOs are central to CSR/EITI. In turn, such good practice codes, regulation and certification can and should be applied to the behavior of actors on all three sides of the Commonwealth "governance" triangle with appropriate recognition from One World Trust and the ISO. Indeed, national and international NGOs are beginning to define, adopt and evaluate their performance, accountability and transparency as indicated in the mid-2006 INGO Accountability Charter agreed by a dozen of the leading agencies, many of whom are Commonwealth-centric: Amnesty International, Civicus, Consumers International, Greenpeace International, Survival International, Transparency International, YMCA, etc.

Meanwhile, states (mainly small) as well as non-state institutions continue to be interested in becoming part of the Commonwealths' family. Thus, as indicated in Chapter 3, the 2005 CHOGM in Malta mandated ComSec to consider possible criteria and forms of future association. Official Commonwealth memberships could come to include those with Associate or Observer status in addition to full, the latter implying some link with an existing Commonwealth member and acceptance and support of Commonwealth values. Such issues, along with questions of multi-cultural communities, identities and faiths, are being deliberated in the run-up to the Commonwealths' summit in Uganda in mid-November 2007 which is to focus on "Transforming Commonwealth Societies." A representative membership committee was appointed in late 2006, chaired by P. J. Patterson, a retired Jamaican prime minister.

One tension this membership committee has to address is that between a more history-based membership criterion (i.e. some association, however tenuous or informal, with the earlier British empire) versus more values-based ones (i.e. compliance with and support for Harare Principles around democratic norms and practices). In turn, the balance between such emphases is somewhat related to whether the Commonwealths are primarily inter- or non-state in orientation. In turn, such a divide reflects more traditional, political, including human rights, emphases versus other priorities such as culture, development, ecology, education, human security, and sport. A related tension may arise between non-member countries that had been part of formal imperialism and those that were sometime incorporated in the informal empire of diplomatic, economic and strategic alliances. The former category includes a finite number of states such as Ireland, Myanmar, Somalia, the United States and Yemen; the latter a more extensive list such as Bahrain, Dubai, Kuwait and UAE in the Gulf; Afghanistan, Egypt, Iraq, Iran, Jordan, Palestine and Sudan in the Middle East; Nepal, and others.

While the Commonwealths contemplate judicious incremental enlargement involving cosmopolitan communities, some largely outside the extended family still envisage a return to imagined good old pre-globalization days of transatlantic insulation and superiority. The Anglosphere Institute has formulated and articulated the latest iteration of an imagined Anglo-American world order. English-speaking cultures, customs and norms still predominate, but have been updated through the exploitation of ICTs. Its US East Coast advocates—white, male, middle-class and middle-aged—still dream of a long-lost anglophone "civilization," one which espouses a capitalist market and civil society throughout the old "white Dominions." These constituted the foundation of the Commonwealth, plus the United States and Ireland, two ex-colonies that have chosen to remain outside ComSec. But the Institute's New England inclinations or romanticism are now modernized through the use of new technologies into a network civilization. Symptomatic of its exclusive, racist inclinations—unlike the contemporary Commonwealths, it has no sense of diasporas and diversities in today's "anglosphere"—it simply allows that "The educated English-speaking populations of the Caribbean, Oceania, Africa and India pertain to the Anglosphere to various degrees."

By contrast, given the Commonwealth's contemporary experience with Harare Principles and members' suspensions, its most recent Expert Group (EG) and development reports are pointers to future foci around the globalization syndrome. First, the Manmohan Singh EG (see Box 5.2) on "Making Democracy Work for Pro-poor Development" called for a new quadrilateral partnership, arguing "that the state, the market, civil society and the international community each has a vital role to play in delivering development and democracy."[3] And second, the report by Stephen Fletcher examined "Challenges to the Commonwealth in Achieving the UN MDGs" with the title of "Poor Commonwealth no Longer?" He concentrated more than the EG on economic than political or social development: competitiveness, globalization, human development and regionalism.

The Manmohan Singh report reflected enlightened, cosmopolitan thinking from eminent analysts from state, civil society and corporate sectors (see Box 5.2 for its dramatis personae) between 9/11 and 7/7. It advocated a four-way partnership amongst governments, firms, civil society and the international community.[4] It also began to identify a segue for the Commonwealths into the problematic yet promising area of diversity and community, concluding with a section on "peace and security" with relevance for the subsequent Amartya Sen Commission on "respect and understanding":

> the Commonwealth could and should be a positive force for celebrating cultural diversity and resisting the advance of fundamentalism and intolerance in every member country.[5]

The Manmohan Singh EG concluded by juxtaposing two dimensions of the contemporary Commonwealths of relevance to their potential contributions to global governance:

> Commonwealth ... should commit to strengthening and encouraging mechanisms for regional conflict resolution and peace-building initiatives through the development of common policy strategies ...
>
> ... appropriate power-sharing arrangements are essential in multiethnic and multicultural societies.
>
> The Expert Group believes ... that the Commonwealth must make more of its comparative advantage with respect to other regional and global bodies. The Commonwealth is a unique microcosm of global social and ethnic diversity, and of North and South. Commonwealth countries and institutions are in a strong position to help deepen democracy and support development in member states.[6]

Yet in a world of more than 200 states, what futures may be identified for the inter- and non-state Commonwealths: more "emerging economies" like India, NICs like Singapore and Malaysia and "developmental states" like Mauritius and Trinidad? Or, rather, "fragile states" like Sri Lanka and Sierra Leone? More INGOs and more MNCs, located in the South as well as the North? And what prospects for a sustainable SIDS regime reinforced by OTs as Associate Members

Table 6.1 Non-independent "Overseas Territories" of Australia, New Zealand and the United Kingdom, 2007

Australian *"External Territories"*	Australian Antarctic Territory*, Ashmore and Cartier Islands*, Christmas Island, Cocos (Keeling) Islands, Coral Sea Islands Territory*, Heard Island and the McDonald Islands*, Norfolk Island
New Zealand *"Associated Countries and External Territories"*	Cook Islands, Niue, Ross Dependency*, Tokelau
UK *"Overseas Territories"*	Anguilla, Bermuda, British Antarctic Territory*, British Indian Ocean Territory*, British Virgin Islands, Cayman Islands, Falkland Islands, Gibraltar, Montserrat, Pitcairn Islands, St. Helena and St. Helena Dependencies, South Georgia and the South Sandwich Islands*, Turks and Caicos Islands

Notes:
* essentially uninhabited by humans *Source*: Richard Green, ed., *Commonwealth Yearbook 2005* (Cambridge: Nexus Strategic Partnerships for Commonwealth Secretariat, 2005): 98–103, 240–46 and 346–67; and *Commonwealth Yearbook 2006*, 19, 113–18, 280–85 and 403–23.

(see Table 6.1)? Are all such projections now overshadowed by the BRICs, especially China and India? Or will more states be reduced to fragile status such as Sierra Leone and Sri Lanka? That is, is the future a generalized China and India, or Africa? And with what implications for the Commonwealths of BRICs and IBSA with their respective Commonwealth dimensions? Three or more worlds?

Alternative futures? Comparative advantages?

The Commonwealth is not growing old, but growing up. It will remain loosely knit, and defined more by shared values than common interests. But the organisation is surprisingly well-suited to help define, deliberate, and develop the international norms, institutions and political will that will enable peace and prosperity to prevail, both within and between Commonwealth members. And it can inspire others.[7]

As I suggested in the Introduction, the two established sides of the Commonwealths hold insights into aspects of global governance, even if analysts have yet to so recognize. I hope that such insights will extend beyond the first decade of the twenty-first century, as new multilateralisms involving broad coalitions of heterogeneous actors are imperative if the growing range of emerging global issues is to be identified and addressed. And I trust I have begun to respond to the timely challenge of Ian Taylor to juxtapose Commonwealths with the conceptual literatures on such new multilateralisms. I therefore have to disagree with the simultaneous assertion of Stephen Chan that:

> the end of the twentieth century and the beginning of the twenty-first, saw a diminution of scholarship on the Commonwealth as an international organization. What was said was either tired or, increasingly, dubious about the Commonwealth—not in terms of its future existence, but in terms of its contemporary effectiveness.[8]

Rather, as David Armstrong suggested in his own helpful overview of possible characterizations or foci of the Commonwealths—community, international organization, small states, good governance, globalization—given its modest resources and status, it may be most effective as "an informal network of networks" which acts as a ginger group in larger alliances and organizations like the EU, IFIs and UN system. He concludes optimistically that given the above series or sequences of "reinventions":

> Alongside the "network of networks" that the Commonwealth still embodies and its lingering community-like features, it would be possible for the Commonwealth to play a role that was both highly valuable and not duplicated by any other IGO.[9]

In short, the above dismissive, negative assertion from Chan is mistaken. Commonwealth practice and related analysis are alive and well in the first decade of the new millennium, as indicated in the lively debate in *Round Table* about the contributions and limitations of the latest book on it by Krishnan Srinivasan, which largely dismisses as well as diminishes any non-state activity or potential.[10]

Like the empire and the British Constitution, the Commonwealths have evolved over time more by happenstance and stealth than planning: the results of changing contexts including competition, memberships, leaderships and coincidences. They did suffer a crisis of confidence as the glory days of the anti-racism struggle concluded along with the end of the Cold War period. That era had been marked by the dominance of non-state actors around the global anti-apartheid movement and the "Third World" charisma of Sonny Ramphal. The 1990s seemed to be a less promising period, symbolized by the more cautious diplomatic style of Emeka Anyaoku (see Box 3.1). However, the combination of the elusiveness of any new world order or peace dividend; failures of successive wars on terrorism; crises in the UN and IFIs and over-expansion of the EU; assertiveness of non-state actors; and the rise of the BRICs along with IBSA together generated an unexpectedly conducive environment for the Commonwealths. Such a "perfect storm" surely requires a return to the undramatic yet necessary and demanding advocacy of human development, human rights and human security.

A set of governmental, civil society and inter-state enquiries in the 1990s—coinciding with the end of bipolarity as well as the Commonwealth's first half-century in 1999—had opened up debate about possible or desirable Commonwealths' futures though its current directions are more by default than design. Like the identification and amelioration of many of today's global policy issues—from global warming to land-mines—they are a function of non-state rather than inter-state agencies, even if not all actors concerned so appreciate or welcome. In this penultimate section, I attempt to juxtapose a trio of overlapping strands—institutional, applied and analytic—which together help to put the contemporary Commonwealths into interrelated organizational, policy and conceptual contexts.

First, institutional development

In the second half of the 1990s, the British parliament and a couple of London-based think tanks held hearings and then reported on the state of the Commonwealth. These were followed by an internal "High Level Review Group" chaired by President Thabo Mbeki of South Africa at the turn of the century which considered possible redirection and reorganization around CHOGM and ComSec between the Durban and Coolum summit. In turn in 2002, a group of Commonwealth organizations produced their own "vision" for the Commonwealths in the twenty-first century before their first summit after 2000, in Brisbane. In terms of the comparative perspective on international organization advanced by Jean-Philippe Therien, most of these reviews tended to opt for a narrower, UN-style intergovernmental approach rather than a broader, nongovernmental purview.[11] Meanwhile, the Commonwealths' brand—nowadays states and cities along with the UN system have logos as well as consumer products—is not as ubiquitous or professionally managed as it might be, in part as most agencies or associations affiliated with the Commonwealths use their own symbol. Hence the timeliness of a discussion at the RCS in London in February 2007 involving advertising agencies: if INGOs now employ brand managers, why not the Commonwealth family?

The House of Commons Commission on the Commonwealth and Mbeki Review Group all tended to treat the Commonwealth as only an inter-state organization rather than an extensive set of overlapping heterogeneous non- as well as intergovernmental networks. They thus focused on improving its institutional structures and international image rather than enhancing its non-state roles and connections. Like Srinivasan, they were preoccupied with intergovernmental decision-making rather than nongovernmental contributions. The Commonwealth organizations' vision was less narrow, calling for more attention to good governance, development, human rights, civil society, youth, and education, with a particular concern for the Commonwealths' image, or lack thereof. And while the Commission on the Commonwealth was largely concerned with the official Commonwealth and with economic relations, it did propose two or three very original ideas, none of which have been taken up elsewhere, especially not by Marlborough House: exchange programs among Commonwealth armed forces; a Commonwealth "university" in the Commonwealth Institute in London; and a Commonwealth yacht to supersede the Queen's decommissioned *Britannia*! The Commission did, however, display foresight in highlighting the potential for the Commonwealths in terms of multi-cultural communication and cooperation:

> The Commonwealth is about diversity ...
> ... (with) increased relevance ... as a network of nations which embraces every religion, many ethnic groups as well as members of every major global multilateral organization. No other group has such a wide range of potential to draw upon.[12]

Second, applied contributions

The pair of reflections and projections from London-based think tanks furthered such broader considerations. The reassessment compiled by Rob Jenkins (1997) for the Royal Institute of International Affairs (RIIA), Commonwealth Parliamentary Association (CPA) and Institute of Commonwealth Studies (ICS) was a response to the above House of Commons report and reflected informed academic, media, policy and political opinion with a focus on inter-regional and North-South linkages, governance and development.[13] While the tone of the Jenkins paper, reflecting the mid-1996 conference deliberations, was skeptical, even cynical, that from the "Blairite" Foreign Policy Centre was more upbeat.

Ford and Katwala presented the broadest and most optimistic perspective, calling for the Commonwealth to be reinvented so that it could advance both globalization and governance. They advocated a "Commonwealth kitemark" or standards logo or seal of approval to indicate compliance with Commonwealth codes. And they emphasized civil society and "the People's Commonwealth," calling for governance rules for NGOs and companies as well as states: a Commonwealth "civil society compact"[14] along the lines of that in the UN. As noted above, in mid-2006, a dozen transatlantic INGOs agreed an INGO Accountability Charter to advance appropriate human resources, effective programs, ethical fundraising, good governance, responsible advocacy, transparency, universal principles, etc. But Ford and Katwala failed to develop extra-Commonwealth notions of diasporas, other than a sentence on page 58 in regard to Commonwealth Games and cultures, which might contribute to more inclusive globalization or human security. I treat these factors in the third part of this section on the Commonwealths' comparative contributions.

In the concluding chapter to his 2001 book *A Guide to the Contemporary Commonwealth*, David McIntyre suggested that the Commonwealth at century's turn and under its fourth secretary-general faced four challenges: "credibility, focus, mechanisms, and balance."[15] These echo many elements identified in the set of contemporary reports mentioned above, though McIntyre goes further than them in his consideration of the non-state dimensions. He notes the recent rise of both people's and corporate Commonwealths by contrast to the established political, or intergovernmental, Commonwealth. And he proceeds to ask whether they are all compatible—"the respective values of the People's and Corporate Commonwealths seem at variance"[16]—and whether "Commonwealth values" or Harare Principles should be extended to the nonofficial dimensions as well as applied to governments. McIntyre also poses a question about the character and acceptability of any "emerging new balance": "In which direction will the long-term balance tilt—public sector, voluntary sector, private sector—IGOs, civil society, business? What are the implications of private-public partnership?"[17]

And finally, third, analytic relevance

Thus far, regrettably, the Commonwealths lack a comprehensive history of the development of their ideas, although many emerged out of inter- and post-war deliberations about decolonization and demobilization, development and multilateralism. The UN Intellectual History

Project (UNIHP) and now Craig Murphy's overview of the UNDP[18] have yet to be replicated for the inter- and non-state Commonwealths. BDEEP and OSPA fall into the tradition of official and unofficial diplomatic histories, respectively, with little reflection on underlying ideas about democracy, development and governance despite some in Commonwealth groups being so concerned. And, unfortunately, Srinivasan's book constitutes more of a personal exegesis about the deficiencies and disinterest of the British government than a dispassionate insider account of the evolution of an international institution. This is particularly regrettable, as his is the only book-length analysis of the Commonwealth to have appeared in the decade to date other than McIntyre's rather empirical, historical overview and Anyaoku's own autobiography (see the very selective, annotated Bibliography at the end of this book).

Especially if one extends the notion of Commonwealths beyond inter-state and formal relations and toward more informal connections around globalization, diasporas, human development and human security, then the Commonwealths may be considered to contribute something distinctive toward definitions and understandings of global governance, as indicated in the opening chapters.

Alternative approaches? Possible projections?

Finally, in a somewhat conjectural conclusion, I would go even further in terms of possible futures for analysis as well as practice—i.e. beyond governance and globalization—by reference to two further analytic approaches or discourses. First, as suggested in Chapter 5 above, the erstwhile "English school" of international relations (IR) might be transcended or globalized by extending it into an emerging "Commonwealth school." In turn, the latter could be seen to have emerged as a distinctive analytic genre from a set of Commonwealth research institutions in addition to myriad Commonwealth universities; in particular, the role of national institutes of international affairs or relations, such as those in Australia, Canada, India, New Zealand, Nigeria, Singapore and South Africa (with a regional, university-based one at the University of the West Indies (UWI)) as well as the UK: previously the Royal Institute of International Affairs, but rebranded in the twenty-first century as Chatham House. The analytic and policy direction of such specifically IR institutions is in turn now increasingly reinforced by other distinctive Commonwealth Plus organizations such as development think tanks like NSI and ODI, advocacy communities like Civitas and Global Witness, and authentic Southern civil society networks like the Aga Khan Foundation, BRAC, Grameen, PRIA, Third World Network, etc.[19]

In turn, such approaches and actors are compatible with the emergence at century's turn of another form of public diplomacy: tracks II and III diplomacy, or semi- or fully private. The title in the Global Institutions series on the World Economic Forum treats such public and private "boundaries," suggesting that the mix of exclusive discussions and access to contemporary ICTs encourages tracks other than the traditional route I, or inter-state. Like the Forum, the Commonwealth, especially its biennial CHOGM, can claim to be "a very private institution with a very public agenda."[20]

And second, relatedly, while the Commonwealths are not just African states, civil societies and companies, their deliberations and activities constitute something of a response to two recent review articles which focus on "African" IR but have a relevance and resonance well beyond that continent. These featured in two major IR journals on either side of the Atlantic which suggested that there is a distinctive African genre of IR. In their readings of contemporary African IR, Douglas Lemke and William Brown argue that traditional state-centrism excludes most of the cross-border relationships on and around the continent that are non-state, informal or illegal.[21] Therefore, for example, analyses of conflict which overlook internal intra-state violence dramatically understate the number of deaths arising from current wars.

Just as Lemke and Brown call for a new IR which can incorporate such "African" realities and data, so I would argue that, to understand the Commonwealths, a more comprehensive, inclusive perspective is likewise imperative, i.e. lessons from Africa for both the rest of the Commonwealths network and the discipline of IR. Without the non-official corporate and peoples' Commonwealths—Commonwealth Plus—the inter-state institution is indeed rather marginal. But once their ubiquitous non-state world is recognized and embraced, especially if in turn the latter is extended to less formal associations with globalizations and diasporas, then the Commonwealths' networks are both more extensive and more efficacious, holding relevance for the generic field of IR.

If so redefined or reconceived, then the Commonwealths are indeed uniquely placed to mediate several antagonistic worlds other than the more familiar North-South, East-West: rich-poor, big-small, island-landlocked, central-marginal, more versus less secular, etc. Encouraged by non-state actors and the several reports indicating possible future policies, new Commonwealth deliberations and directions should be anticipated at successive CHOGMs and CPFs as outlined in the previous pair of chapters. Hopefully, following the late-2009 summit in Trinidad, the Commonwealths in the next decade will advance toward collaboration, cosmopolitanism, and convergence instead of conflict, difference, and divergence as encouraged by the Manmohan Singh Expert Group.

In turn, such directions are likely to be reinforced by the present deliberations of and proposals from the Amartya Sen Commission on respect and understanding.

Commonwealth diplomacy and governance—the "triangle" of governmental, corporate and civil society—increasingly now depends on Blackberries, the handheld communications device from Research in Motion (RIM), themselves in part a function of Canada being a leader in telecommunications for obvious geographical reasons. And RIM has given generously to the new Center for International Governance Innovation (CIGI) at the University of Waterloo, in Canada's high-tech region of Southern Ontario, which seeks to advance an innovative Canada-centric set of global governance scenarios for the world of today and tomorrow. As suggested in this book, the Commonwealths can contribute to such visions, given their unique mix of local and global, community and corporate perspectives.

Finally, and more speculatively and academically or abstractly, as already suggested, given the Commonwealths' particular mix of actors and values, might its set of institutes of IR as identified in the previous section come to define a distinctive approach to the field: a "Commonwealth school of IR" to supersede or parallel the erstwhile English school? In turn, they might also juxtapose or combine insights from several overlapping discourses around African IR, CIGI, etc. Together, these largely compatible strands might then come to identify and define novel versions of global governance and new multilateralisms for human development, human rights and human security into the second decade of the twenty-first century, following an unexpectedly troubled first decade. Such inclusive directions or projections stand in rather stark and welcome contrast to the dominant and exclusive unilateral scenario advanced by the one remaining global superpower, the United States. They would indicate and vindicate the comparative contributions arising from contemporary Commonwealths as the second decade of the new century approaches.

In short, as anticipated in this book's opening chapter, the Commonwealths, as a microcosm, can reveal aspects of comparative global governance. They can advance insights drawn from a variety of analytic perspectives, not just international law, international organization and international relations, as indicated, somewhat optimistically, in the Introduction.

Appendix 1

Official Commonwealth membership and year of joining

Pre-1945	Australia, Britain, Canada, India, New Zealand, South Africa
1947	Pakistan
1955	Ceylon (Sri Lanka from 1972)
1957	Ghana, Malaya (Malaysia from 1963)
1960	Cyprus, Nigeria
1961	Sierra Leone, Tanganyika (Tanzania from 1964)
1962	Jamaica, Trinidad, Uganda
1963	Kenya
1964	Malawi, Malta, Zambia
1965	Gambia, Maldives, Singapore
1966	Barbados, Botswana, Guyana, Lesotho
1968	Mauritius, Swaziland, Nauru (special member)
1970	Fiji, Tonga, Western Somoa
1972	Bangladesh
1973	Bahamas
1974	Grenada
1975	Papua New Guinea
1976	Seychelles
1978	Dominica, Solomon Islands, Tuvalu (special member)
1979	Kiribati, St. Lucia, St. Vincent (special member)
1980	St. Vincent, Zimbabwe
1981	Antigua, Belize, Vanuatu
1983	St. Kitts-Nevis
1984	Brunei
1990	Namibia
1994	South Africa (return after withdrawal in 1961)
1995	Cameroon, Mozambique

(David McIntyre, *A Guide to the Contemporary Commonwealth*, London: Palgrave, 2001, 114–15, and Richard Green, ed., *The Commonwealth Yearbook 2006*, 20. NB The members are also listed, in sequence of joining, in the brochure of the annual Commonwealth Day service held in Westminster Abbey.)

Appendix 2
CHOGM location, participation and duration, 1965–2009

Date	Location	Participation	Days duration
1965	London	21	9
1966	Lagos (January)	19	3
1966	London (Sept)	22	10
1969	London	28	9
1971	Singapore	31	9
1973	Ottawa	32	9
1975	Kingston	33	8
1977	London	34	8
1979	Lusaka	39	7
1981	Melbourne	42	8
1983	New Delhi	42	7
1985	Nassau	46	7
1987	Vancouver	45	5
1989	Kuala Lumpur	46	7
1991	Harare	47	7
1993	Limassol	47	5
1995	Auckland	48	3.5
1997	Edinburgh	51	3.5
1999	Durban	52	3.5
2002	Coolum		
2003	Abuja		3
2005	Malta	53	2.5
2007	Kampala		
2009	Trinidad		

Source: David McIntyre, *A Guide to the Contemporary Commonwealth* (London: Palgrave, 2001), 85. See also "Biennial Summits," in *The Commonwealth Yearbook 2006*, ed. Richard Green (Cambridge: Nexus for ComSec, 2006), 47–60.

Appendix 3
Commonwealth organizations

Intergovernmental

Commonwealth Foundation (1965)

www.commonwealthfoundation.com: To facilitate the development of civil societies and professional associations throughout the Commonwealth including the organization of the biennial Commonwealth People's Forum which coincides with and complements CHOGM.

Commonwealth of Learning (1987)

www.col.org: To advance distance education and open learning knowledge, resources and technologies throughout the Commonwealth.

Commonwealth Secretariat (ComSec) (1965)

www.thecommonwealth.org: The primary intergovernmental agency of the Commonwealth to facilitate inter-state consultation, cooperation, and consensus.

Commonwealth Telecommunications Organization

www.cto.org: A global development partnership between Commonwealth and non-Commonwealth governments, companies and civil societies to employ information and communications technologies (ICTs) to bridge the digital divide.

Commonwealth Youth Programme

www.thecommonwealth.org/cyp: To assist members with programming that empowers youth especially through its four regional centers in Africa (Zambia), Asia (India), Caribbean (Guyana) and South Pacific (Solomon Islands).

Nongovernmental

Association for Commonwealth Literature and Language Studies (ACLALS)

www.aclals.org: An association of academics and writers to promote the study and analysis of Commonwealth literatures and languages.

Association of Commonwealth Universities (1913)

www.acu.ac.uk: A voluntary association of 500 universities throughout the Commonwealth to advance cooperation in higher education.

Commonwealth Business Council (1997)

www.cbcglobelink.org: A membership organization of about 200 corporations in the Commonwealth which promotes regional and sectoral forums and public-private partnerships, including Commonwealth Business Forums around biennial CHOGMs.

Commonwealth Games Federation (1930)

www.thecgf.com: A federation of over 70 national games associations who compete every four years between the Olympic summer games, increasingly with corporate sponsorships, which now also supports the development of the Commonwealth Youth Games.

Commonwealth Human Rights Initiative (1987)

www.humanrightsinitiative.org: An INGO founded by other Commonwealth associations based in New Delhi which advances human rights, especially through biennial human rights reports and forums around CHOGMs.

Commonwealth Journalists' Association (1978)

www.cjaweb.com: A Trinidad-based professional association to advance standards and rights of journalism in the Commonwealth through education and advocacy.

Commonwealth Lawyers' Association (1983)

www.commonwealthlawyers.com: A professional association to promote the rule of law throughout the Commonwealth initially established in

1986. Its jubilee conference was in London in September 2005. It collaborates closely with the Commonwealth Judges and Magistrates Association.

Commonwealth Local Government Forum (1995)

www.clgf.org.uk: A forum to encourage good democratic local governance by governments and other private and public agencies through biennial conferences and annual handbooks of best practice.

Commonwealth Medical Association (1962)

A Commonwealth grouping of national medical associations to encourage medical education and ethics in collaboration with the WHO.

Commonwealth Parliamentary Association (1911)

www.cpahq.org: The association for some 15,000 members of national and state/provincial parliaments in 175 branches throughout the Commonwealth; it encourages best democratic practices through an annual conference and inter-parliamentary exchanges.

Commonwealth Press Union (1909)

www.cpu.org.uk: The post-1950 incarnation of an imperial network with over 800 newspaper groups and organizations to defend freedom of the press and provide professional training.

Commonwealth Scholarship and Fellowship Plan (1959)

www.csfp-online.org: An umbrella of some 15 national scholarship schemes to facilitate interdisciplinary postgraduate education in the Commonwealth; it already boasts over 23,000 alumni.

Royal Commonwealth Society (1868)

www.rcsint.org: A Commonwealth-wide NGO of 6,000 direct members and 10,000 other members in affiliated branches in over 40 countries renamed in 1958; it advances debates and communication and organizes an annual Commonwealth Essay Competition (over a century old, receiving some 5,000 entries each year) and Commonwealth Day events and theme.

Commonwealth Plus

Aga Khan Foundation/Development Network

www.akdn.org: A private international development agency committed to supporting disadvantaged communities irrespective of gender, ethnicity or religion, which works in partnership with local organizations and communities to promote solutions for social and economic development in Central Asia, South Asia and Eastern Africa.

Other prominent organizations

British Broadcasting Corporation (www.bbc.com)
British Council (www.britishcouncil.org)
CABI International (www.cabi.org)
English Speaking Union (1918) (www.esu.org)
Oxfam (www.oxfam.org)
Save the Children (www.scf.org)
Voluntary Service Overseas (www.vso.org)

(See Richard Green, ed., *The Commonwealth Yearbook 2005*: 405–36, and David McIntyre, *A Guide to the Contemporary Commonwealth* (London: Palgrave, 2001), 163–75.)

Appendix 4
The Malta Communiqué

Commonwealth Heads of Government Meeting, Malta, 25–27 November 2005

Final communiqué

1 Commonwealth Heads of Government met in Malta from 25 to 27 November 2005. Of the 52 countries that attended the Meeting, 38 were represented by their Heads of State or Government.

2 The Opening Ceremony of the Meeting included an address by Her Majesty Queen Elizabeth II, Head of the Commonwealth.

3 Heads of Government conveyed their sincere appreciation to the Government and people of Malta for the warm hospitality extended to them and for the excellent arrangements made for the Meeting. They also congratulated Prime Minister Lawrence Gonzi for his leadership in chairing the Meeting.

4 Noting that their Meeting was taking place following the United Nations 2005 World Summit, Heads of Government reaffirmed their commitment to the outcome of this Summit.

Fundamental political values

5 Heads of Government reaffirmed their commitment to the Commonwealth's fundamental political values of tolerance, respect, international peace and security, democracy, good governance, human rights, gender equality, rule of law, the independence of the judiciary, freedom of expression, and a political culture that promotes transparency, accountability and economic development.

6 Heads of Government expressed their full support for the good offices role of the Secretary-General in conflict prevention and resolution, and post-conflict reconstruction and development. They also expressed their continuing commitment to the Commonwealth Secretariat's work for strengthening democratic institutions, processes and culture including through election observation, provision

of technical assistance and training and other activities, upon the request of the countries concerned.

7   Heads of Government welcomed the Secretariat's collaboration with the Commonwealth Parliamentary Association (CPA), the Commonwealth Local Government Forum (CLGF) and other relevant organisations to promote best democratic practice. They commended the CPA for providing assistance to Commonwealth Parliaments for capacity building and promoting awareness about the respective roles of the Government and Opposition in democracies. They also noted the outcomes of the CLGF Conference in 2005, and in this context welcomed the Aberdeen Agenda.

Commonwealth principles on good practice for local democracy and good governance.

8   Heads of Government noted that the Commonwealth (Latimer House) Principles on the Accountability of and Relationship between the Three Branches of Government 2003, which recognise the importance of a balance of power between the Executive, Legislature and Judiciary, constitute an integral part of the Commonwealth's fundamental political values as set out in the Harare Commonwealth Declaration.

Commonwealth Ministerial Action Group on the Harare Declaration (CMAG)

9   Heads of Government endorsed the Report of the Commonwealth Ministerial Action Group on the Harare Declaration (CMAG) covering the Group's deliberations in the period since the Abuja Commonwealth Heads of Government Meeting in December 2003. They commended CMAG's work which has contributed significantly to the promotion of the Commonwealth's fundamental political values in member countries.

10   Heads of Government expressed sympathy with the Government and people of Pakistan for the massive loss of life and devastation caused by the earthquake in October 2005.

11   Heads of Government welcomed the progress made by Pakistan in restoring democracy and rebuilding democratic institutions as well as Pakistan's participation in the Commonwealth since its reinstatement by CMAG in May 2004.

12   Heads of Government noted that the holding by the same person of the offices of Head of State and Chief of Army Staff is incompatible

with the basic principles of democracy and the spirit of the Harare Commonwealth principles. They reiterated that until the two offices are separated, the process of democratisation in Pakistan will not be irreversible.

13 Heads of Government urged Pakistan to resolve this issue as early as possible, and not beyond the end of the current Presidential term in 2007 at the latest. They noted that CMAG will retain Pakistan on its agenda pending the resolution of this outstanding issue.

14 Heads of Government requested the Secretary-General to continue to maintain high level contacts with Pakistan and utilise his good offices and technical assistance, as appropriate, to support the strengthening of democracy, institution building and democratic governance.

15 Heads of Government reconstituted the membership of CMAG for the next biennium as follows: Canada, Lesotho, Malaysia, Papua New Guinea, St Lucia, Sri Lanka, United Kingdom and United Republic of Tanzania. They further agreed that Malta would continue to be a member of CMAG in its capacity as the representative of the Chairperson in Office, as its ninth member.

Belize

16 Heads of Government noted the developments in the continuing efforts of Belize to bring an end to Guatemala's territorial claim, including the Agreement on a Framework for Negotiations and Confidence Building Measures between Belize and Guatemala signed by the two Parties and the Secretary General of the Organisation of American States (OAS) on 7 September 2005. Heads of Government noted that this Agreement provided for a mechanism to allow recourse to an international judicial body for final resolution should the parties fail to reach agreement in negotiations, and expressed the confidence that this framework could bring this long-lasting claim to an early end. Heads of Government reiterated their firm support for the territorial integrity, security and sovereignty of Belize.

17 Heads of Government mandated the Secretary-General to convene the Ministerial Committee on Belize, whenever necessary.

Cyprus

18 Reaffirming their previous Communiqués on Cyprus, Heads of Government expressed their support for the sovereignty, independence, territorial integrity and unity of the Republic of Cyprus.

19   They welcomed the accession of the Republic of Cyprus to the European Union. They expressed their support for a lasting, just and functional settlement based on the principles of the United Nations Charter, the relevant UN Security Council resolutions and the principles of the Commonwealth.

20   Heads of Government called for the implementation of UN Security Council Resolutions on Cyprus, in particular Security Council Resolutions 365 (1974), 541 (1983), 550 (1984), 1250 (1999) and all subsequent resolutions. They reiterated their support for the respect for the human rights of all Cypriots, including the right to property, the implementation of the relevant decisions of the European Court of Human Rights and for the accounting for all missing persons.

21   Heads of Government further agreed on the importance of supporting the efforts of the UN Secretary-General to bring about a comprehensive settlement of the Cyprus problem in line with relevant UN Security Council Resolutions.

Guyana

22   Heads of Government noted that the Commonwealth Ministerial Group on Guyana which was established in 1999 to monitor developments in respect of the existing controversy between Guyana and Venezuela met recently in September 2005.

23   Heads of Government expressed satisfaction at the cordiality which had characterised relations between Guyana and Venezuela in recent years and recognised the instrumental role of dialogue at the highest levels in facilitating the commitment to a peaceful settlement of the controversy under the aegis of the UN Good Offices Process and to enhanced co-operation at the bilateral, regional and multilateral levels.

24   Heads of Government reaffirmed their unequivocal support for the maintenance of Guyana's territorial integrity and sovereignty including its unrestricted right to the development of the entirety of its territory for the benefit of its people.

25   Heads of Government mandated the Secretary-General to convene the Ministerial Group on Guyana, whenever necessary.

Promoting tolerance and respect

26   Heads of Government affirmed the importance of promoting tolerance, respect, enlightened moderation and friendship among people of different races, faiths and cultures. In this regard they commended various initiatives at the national, regional and international

level and encouraged the Commonwealth Secretariat to strengthen its interaction with other bodies that seek to build a common platform of unity against extremism and intolerance. Heads of Government also requested the Secretary-General to explore initiatives to promote mutual understanding and respect among all faiths and communities in the Commonwealth.

Peace and security

27 Heads of Government observed that insecurity, armed conflict, gender inequality and the failure to promote and protect human rights undermine development and poverty reduction and endanger the security and stability of states. They underlined that social and economic marginalisation also undermines security and stability. Heads of Government urged member countries to ensure that, where appropriate, national poverty reduction frameworks and development assistance programmes include measures to build effective and accountable security and justice sectors, particularly in countries affected by conflicts.

28 Heads of Government acknowledged the threats posed by weapons of mass destruction and in this regard reaffirmed their commitments towards the attainment of general and complete disarmament including nuclear disarmament. They also reaffirmed their commitment to the non-proliferation of weapons of mass destruction. They reiterated that these objectives should be achieved in accordance with the United Nations Charter.

29 Heads of Government noted the substantive contributions of Commonwealth members to peace building and to UN peace support operations, as major troop contributors and donors. They reaffirmed the decision by the UN 2005 World Summit to establish a Peace Building Commission, a Support Office and Fund to co-ordinate relevant actors and advise on integrated strategies for post-conflict reconstruction so as to lay the foundation for sustainable peace and development. They urged that these bodies be established by the end of 2005 and called for active Commonwealth collaboration with the Peace Building Commission to provide support for post-conflict reconstruction.

Terrorism

30 Heads of Government reaffirmed their strong condemnation of all acts of terrorism in all its forms and manifestations and

recognised that terrorism continues to present a serious challenge to international peace and security. They emphasised that targeting and deliberate killing of civilians through acts of terrorism cannot be justified or legitimised by any cause or grievance.

31 Heads of Government stressed the continuing need for comprehensive efforts at local, national, regional and international levels, to counter terrorism, which also take into account the conditions conducive to the spread of terrorism. In this context, they commended the various initiatives to promote dialogue, tolerance and understanding among civilisations.

32 Heads of Government also called for increased efforts to promote economic development and good governance as a means of tackling insecurity and conflict. They recognised that international cooperation to fight terrorism must be conducted in conformity with international law, including the UN Charter and relevant international conventions and protocols. States must ensure that measures taken to combat terrorism comply with their obligations under international law, in particular human rights law, refugee law and international humanitarian law.

33 Heads of Government called upon all states to accede to and effectively implement the UN Conventions and Protocols related to terrorism. They reiterated the need for all states to tackle the financing of, incitement to, and other support for terrorist activities and to take appropriate measures, including the effective implementation of the relevant UN Security Council Resolutions, to ensure that their territories are not used for such activities. Heads of Government stressed the need to conclude a Comprehensive Convention on International Terrorism during the sixtieth session of the UN General Assembly, and support the early entry into force of the International Convention for the Suppression of Acts of Nuclear Terrorism.

34 Heads of Government encouraged all member governments to continue to follow steps outlined in the Commonwealth Plan of Action and to implement UNSCR 1373 (2001) and relevant UN and other international resolutions, conventions and standards aimed at combating terrorism. In this context they commended the work of the Commonwealth Secretariat in assisting member countries and reiterated the need to further strengthen counter-terrorism co-operation and assistance, particularly in the area of capacity-building.

United Nations reform

35 Heads of Government reiterated the need to build a UN fit to
meet the challenges of the 21st century. They called for urgent
reforms in the UN decision-making structure, including the
expansion of the Security Council, to make the UN system more
broadly representative, efficient and transparent, to further enhance
its effectiveness and the legitimacy and implementation of its
decisions. Heads of Government also underlined the vital importance of an effective multilateral system based on the principles of
international law, in order to achieve progress in the areas of
peace and security, development and human rights. This should
include action to strengthen the management and coherence of
the UN humanitarian and development systems, so that the UN
can fulfil its potential to help accelerate progress towards attainment of the MDGs. They agreed to actively follow up the outcomes of the UN 2005 World Summit.

Responsibility to protect

36 Heads of Government welcomed the universal acceptance at the
UN 2005 World Summit that each individual state has the
responsibility to protect its population from genocide, war
crimes, ethnic cleansing and crimes against humanity. This
responsibility entails the prevention of such crimes, including
their incitement, through appropriate and necessary means. They
urged Commonwealth countries to help states to exercise this
responsibility and support the UN in establishing an early warning capability. They welcomed the recognition that the responsibility to protect populations from genocide, warcrimes, ethnic
cleansing and crimes against humanity is also a collective responsibility, through the UN and bearing in mind the principles of the
UN Charter and international law, should peaceful means be
inadequate and national authorities are manifestly failing to protect their populations.

37 Heads of Government agreed that the responsibility and obliga-
tion to protect populations from such acts is a fundamental
Commonwealth value, consistent with Commonwealth commitments to human rights, democracy, good governance and international law. They agreed to work together to ensure that the
responsibility to protect is carried out by the international community, in accordance with the UN Charter.

International Criminal Court

38   Heads of Government of those member countries that have ratified the Rome Statute establishing the International Criminal Court welcomed the 100th ratification the Rome Statute and urged other states that have not yet done so to accede to the Rome Statute in a timely manner.

Small arms and light weapons

39   Heads of Government expressed their deep concern over the illicit production, illegal trade and uncontrolled availability of small arms and light weapons, which prolong conflict, increase levels of armed violence and undermine development. They acknowledged the nexus between drug trafficking, illegal trade in small arms, organised crime and terrorism and stressed the need for continued regional and international collaboration to combat these threats. Heads of Government noted the proposals by certain member states for the establishment of common international standards for the transfer of small arms and light weapons. They urged all member states to support the strengthening of the UN Programme of Action on Small Arms and Light Weapons.

40   Heads of Government further expressed their deep concern at the recruitment and use of children in armed conflict by armed forces and groups and urged member states to take measures to ensure accountability by those responsible for abuse against children and to prohibit and criminalise such practices and assist those affected children.

Arms trade treaty

41   Heads of Government noted the proposal for the development of common international standards for the trade in all conventional weapons and added their support to calls for work on such a treaty to commence at the UN.

Drug trafficking and transnational crime

42   Heads of Government recognised that drug trafficking and related transnational criminal activities are serious threats to stability, security and development. They emphasised the need for all countries, particularly producing, consuming and transit countries, to continue to work together bilaterally and multilaterally to fight the harmful effects of drug trafficking.

43 Heads of Government expressed concern that transnational crime is a serious and growing threat to Commonwealth jurisdictions, especially those small states which might experience resource constraints and capacity issues to respond effectively.

Landmines

44 Heads of Government recalled the progress made by States party to the Ottawa Convention on the Prohibition of the Use, Stockpiling, Production and Transfer of Anti-Personnel Mines and on their Destruction in addressing the global anti-personnel landmines problem through the Comprehensive Framework for Mine Action provided by the Convention. They urged all countries which are in a position to do so, to accede to the Convention and fully implement their respective obligations. They recognised the importance of the continuation of the international community's assistance for affected countries aimed at achieving the goals established by the Ottawa Convention by 2009.

Human rights

45 Heads of Government commended the Secretariat's work in assisting member countries to promote and protect human rights and fundamental freedoms as enshrined in the Universal Declaration of Human Rights and other relevant instruments. They reaffirmed that respect for and protection of civil, political, economic, social and cultural rights, including the right to development, is the foundation of peaceful, just and stable societies and that these rights are universal, indivisible, interdependent and inter-related. In this context, they welcomed the agreement reached by the UN 2005 World Summit to establish a Human Rights Council. Heads of Government urged member countries to conduct open, transparent and inclusive negotiations to be completed as soon as possible during the sixtieth session of the UN General Assembly with the aim of establishing the mandate, modalities, functions, size, composition, membership, working methods and procedures of the Council.

Public financial management reform

46 Heads of Government welcomed the guidelines for Public Financial Management Reform considered by the Commonwealth

Finance Ministers in Barbados in September 2005 and urged member Governments to devise suitable measures to adopt and implement these guidelines to support the reform of this important sector. Heads of Government appreciated the work of the Commonwealth Association for Public Administration and Management (CAPAM) in governance, public administration and public sector reform.

Combating corruption

47   Heads of Government reiterated their commitment to root out, both at national and international levels, systemic corruption, including extortion and bribery, which undermine good governance, respect for human rights and economic development. They acknowledged that comprehensive preventative measures, including institutionalising transparency, accountability and good governance, combined with effective enforcement, are the most effective means to combat corruption.

48   Heads of Government welcomed the imminent entry into force of the UN Convention against Corruption and urged member states which had not already done so to become parties to the Convention and to strengthen the fight against corruption by the adoption of principles and policies, as appropriate, that emphasise good governance, accountability and transparency.

Recovery and repatriation of assets of illicit origin

49   Heads of Government accepted for implementation the recommendations of the Report of the Commonwealth Expert Group on the Recovery and Repatriation of Assets of Illicit Origin. Corruption, reprehensible as it is, should not, however, be equated with war crimes or genocide. Heads of Government underscored the importance of maximum cooperation and assistance by all Commonwealth countries to recover assets of illicit origin and repatriate them to their countries of origin.

Migration and development

50   Heads of Government underlined the need to deal with the challenges and opportunities that migration presents to countries of origin, destination and transit. In an interconnected world, growth and prosperity increasingly rely on the global flow of people, for

travel, work and study. When managed effectively migration can have a substantial positive impact both for host and source countries and for migrants. Heads of Government emphasized that better management of migration flows is a matter of priority. They urged member countries to participate actively in the UN High-Level Dialogue on International Migration and Development in 2006 to deliberate its multidimensional aspects. Heads of Government also reaffirmed their resolve to take measures to ensure respect for and protection of the human rights of migrants, migrant workers and members of their families, as enshrined in international law.

Human trafficking

51 Heads of Government condemned human trafficking which deprives people of their human dignity, including their fundamental rights and freedoms. They acknowledged that eradicating human trafficking requires a comprehensive approach which focuses on prevention, protection and prosecution. Heads of Government urged member states to honour all obligations arising under international law and to support the full implementation of the 2000 Protocol to Prevent, Suppress and Punish Trafficking in Persons, Especially Women and Children, Supplementing the UN Convention Against Transnational Organised Crime. Heads of Government also affirmed the principle of solidarity and burden-sharing with regard to assistance of refugees and their host communities.

Digital divide

52 Heads of Government highlighted the significant potential contribution of information and communication technologies for development and issued the *Malta Commonwealth Declaration on Networking for Development.*

Commonwealth Fund for Technical Co-operation (CFTC)

53 Heads of Government expressed their appreciation for the CFTC's programme of assistance in the areas of debt management, trade development and investment promotion, as well as in governance, public sector development, gender equality, human development, and in addressing anti-money laundering issues.

54 They expressed their concern at the progressive decline in the real resources of the CFTC over the years and noted that this was affecting its ability to assist member countries, especially Small States and Least Developed Countries (LDCs), to attain the MDGs by supporting pro-poor policies for economic growth and sustainable development. They endorsed the support expressed at the Commonwealth Finance Ministers Meeting in Barbados in September 2005 for the Secretary-General's call on all member Governments to increase contributions to the CFTC by 6 per cent per annum in real terms for each of the next five years. Heads of Government also welcomed recent substantial increases in pledges to the CFTC by some countries and urged other member countries to do likewise. They also welcomed the continued efforts by individual member countries in extending technical assistance to other member countries within and outside the framework of the CFTC.

World economic situation

55 Heads of Government welcomed the ongoing global expansion and low levels of inflation. However, they noted that unbalanced growth, disparities in global current accounts and savings, high and volatile oil prices, increasing protectionist sentiments and the effects of natural disasters continue to impact negatively on the outlook and urged concerted international efforts to minimise these major sources of risk.

56 Heads of Government emphasised that oil producers and consumers as well as oil companies need to work together to promote greater transparency and stability in the oil market and enhance access to energy, including alternative sources of energy, and also to assist the poor and most vulnerable countries to deal with the impact of rising energy prices.

Meeting the Millennium Development Goals

57 Heads of Government expressed deep concern that many Commonwealth countries were falling behind the MDG targets. They noted that the MDGs were largely linked to poverty reduction, health, education and gender equality targets, and urged member countries to re-commit themselves to human development. Heads of Government noted with satisfaction the achievement of some of the MDGs by some member countries. They called

upon all member countries to continue to pursue macro-economic stability and to strengthen the social and economic policies and human rights frameworks needed for sustainable growth and poverty reduction. They also urged the international community, led by developed countries, to follow through expeditiously on commitments regarding Official Development Assistance (ODA) and debt, particularly for LDCs and low-income countries.

58 Heads of Government welcomed the increased resources that will become available as a result of the establishment of timetables by many developed countries to achieve the target of 0.7 per cent of gross national product (GNP) for ODA by 2015 and to reach at least 0.5 per cent of GNP for ODA by 2010 as well as, pursuant to the Brussels Programme of Action for the LDCs, 0.15 per cent to 0.20 per cent for the LDCs by no later than 2010, and urged those developed countries that have not yet done so to make concrete efforts in this regard in accordance with their commitments. They urged others to continue to take concrete steps towards reaching this goal in accordance with their commitments. They also welcomed greater attention paid to the priority issues of vaccination and immunisation, including the decision by some countries to launch the International Finance Facility for Immunisation (IFFIm) and plans to implement new voluntary mechanisms to generate additional and predictable aid resources. Heads of Government requested the Secretary-General to include information on action taken to implement ODA commitments in the documentation for their next meeting.

59 Heads of Government recognised that along with increases in volumes, aid needs to be made more effective. In this regard, they called for determined action by all countries to implement the commitments made in the 2005 Paris Declaration on Aid. They also stressed the need to respect national processes in setting and implementing development strategies, and for donors to align their support with national priorities.

60 Heads of Government noted that some middle-income countries continue to face mounting debt problems, challenges in respect of the negative impact of HIV/AIDS, vulnerability to natural disasters, high unemployment and prevailing poverty. They noted that middle-income countries contain 70 per cent of the world population earning less than two dollars a day and continued to face development challenges.

Multilateral trade issues

61   Heads of Government emphasised that increased trading opportunities were the most potent weapon for combating global poverty. They issued the *Valletta Statement on Multilateral Trade.*

Debt relief

62   Heads of Government noted the vanguard role played by the UK Government and welcomed the proposal of the G8 countries for a fully funded 100 per cent debt cancellation for eligible Heavily Indebted Poor Countries (HIPC) on their debt to International Development Association (IDA), International Monetary Fund (IMF) and the African Development Fund (AfDF). They called on shareholders to support full and immediate action to implement these proposals. Once approved, consideration could be given to the extension of the initiative to debt owed to other multilateral institutions. In addition, they noted that it is important that the cancellation of multilateral debt does not compromise the financing capacity of the institutions involved and that IDA debt does not compromise the target of 50 per cent of IDA 14 funds being spent in sub-Saharan African countries pursuing sound policies, consistent with the IDA 14 final report.

63   Heads of Government expressed their shared concern about the effectiveness of the use of resources released through debt cancellation. They stressed that current programmes were able to ensure this without the need for additional conditionality. They called on the Bretton Woods Institutions to ensure that the debt sustainability framework is aligned to the achievement of the MDGs.

64   Heads of Government further stressed the need to consider additional measures and initiatives aimed at ensuring long term debt sustainability through increased grant based financing, cancellation of 100 per cent of the official multilateral and bilateral debt of Heavily Indebted Poor Countries (HIPC) and, where appropriate, and on a case-by-case basis, to consider significant debt relief or restructuring for low- and middle-income developing countries, including Least Developed Countries, with an unsustainable debt burden that are not part of the HIPC Initiative, as well as the exploration of mechanisms to comprehensively address the debt problems of these countries.

Investment

65 Heads of Government noted the importance of productive investment and the financial sectors as building blocks for economic growth, resource mobilisation and eradication of poverty. They recognised that improvements in the investment climate reduce investor costs and risks and generate higher rates of private sector investment and sustainable economic growth. Heads of Government called for increased efforts to address shortcomings in the investment climate, including the overall regulatory environment, in order to attract greater levels of both domestic and foreign investment. Heads of Government further noted that easy access to financial services by poor people reduces risk and vulnerability and increases income potential, and that new focus needs to be given to removing barriers to wider provision of services by banks and other commercial providers. They called for the adoption of financial access indicators to help guide reform and monitor progress.

Strengthening financial systems

66 Heads of Government welcomed developments within the recent meeting of the Organisation for Economic Cooperation and Development (OECD) Global Forum, which focused on the issue of a global level playing field and fairness in the area of transparency and information exchange in tax matters and stressed that the way forward required a satisfactory resolution of this issue. They also welcomed the continued engagement of the Commonwealth on this issue, which, through the Secretariat, has offered support to a number of the affected jurisdictions by mobilizing assistance to meet international standards, strengthen and deepen their financial sectors and diversify their economies.

67 Heads of Government also commended the Commonwealth Secretariat for the technical assistance it is currently providing to the International Trade and Investment Organisation (ITIO).

New Partnership for Africa's Development (NEPAD)

68 Heads of Government recognised that poverty and underdevelopment continue to challenge many African member countries in meeting the MDGs. They reiterated their support for the

initiative taken by African leaders in setting up the NEPAD, and the African Peer Review Mechanism (APRM) and stressed their positive role in promoting economic development, good governance, democratic institutions and practices.

69 Heads of Government requested the Commonwealth Secretariat to continue bringing its various programmes in Africa within the NEPAD framework and to strengthen its partnership with AU/NEPAD. They also requested the Secretariat to consider support for its African Priority Programmes and Needs as identified at the Africa Partnership Forum and in the Report of the Commission for Africa.

Sustainable development

70 Heads of Government noted with concern the adverse immediate and long term effects of climate change, biodiversity loss, water management issues, deforestation and sea-level rise on small island and other states that are particularly vulnerable to the impacts of global warming and sea level rise. They urged Commonwealth member states and the wider international community to meet their obligations under relevant multilateral environment agreements including the UN Framework Convention on Climate Change (UNFCCC) and to implement their commitments under Agenda 21 and the Johannesburg Plan of Implementation (JPOI).

71 Heads of Government called for co-operation and continued international efforts to address the specific challenges posed by climate change, in accordance with the principle of common but differentiated responsibilities and adaptation, including capacity building, and saw a role for the Commonwealth in progressing this agenda. They also called for international co-operation in addressing issues related to the transfer of affordable technologies and the management and promotion of renewable energy resources. Heads of Government also stressed the importance of the eleventh session of the Conference of the Parties to the UNFCCC, to be held in Montreal in November 2005.

72 To this end, Heads of Government acknowledged the role of some Commonwealth member states in the development of positive initiatives on climate change and sustainable development, including the G8 dialogue on Climate Change, Clean Energy and Sustainable Development and the Asia Pacific Partnership on Clean Development and Climate.

73 Heads of Government recognised the importance of the role of the Commonwealth Iwokrama Rainforest Programme in Guyana in conserving and sustainably utilising tropical rainforest resources. They drew attention to the need for funding to be made available to secure the future of the Programme over the long term. They also welcomed the initiatives of the Papua New Guinea Government on climate change and rainforests.

Small states

74 Heads of Government reaffirmed their commitment to small states, recognising their particular challenges and vulnerabilities. They issued the *Gozo Statement on Vulnerable Small States*.

Natural disasters and humanitarian assistance

75 Heads of Government noted with concern the devastating and increasing impact of natural and man-made disasters on human lives, infrastructure and economies. They called for action at the national, regional and international levels to strengthen disaster management through increased capacity for disaster preparedness, early warning systems, risk mitigation and post-disaster recovery and reconstruction. In this context, they welcomed the proposal to develop a Commonwealth Programme for Natural Disaster Management, through which member countries could cooperate in capacity building for disaster risk reduction and disaster response management. They requested the Secretary General to develop a mechanism for establishing and operationalising the proposed initiative in consultation with member states.

76 Heads of Government emphasised the critical importance of effective, timely and equitable humanitarian action in support of disaster affected populations. In this regard, they called on member countries to support efforts to further strengthen the international humanitarian response system, including the proposed extension of the UN Central Emergency Revolving Fund and the strengthening of the UN humanitarian coordination system. They noted that international strategies for disaster reduction should take due cognisance of national policies and establish partnerships upon the request of countries concerned so as to support and complement the national programmes of affected countries.

Health and HIV/AIDS

77 Heads of Government reaffirmed their commitment to combating HIV/AIDS, malaria, tuberculosis and other communicable diseases, which all threaten sustainable development. They acknowledged that LDCs, Small Island Developing States (SIDS) and other vulnerable states face particular difficulties in responding to HIV/AIDS and other major diseases, and in reaching the goal of universal access to prevention, treatment, care and support for HIV/AIDS by 2010. They urged the Secretariat to continue to assist countries with prevention measures and strengthening health systems.

78 Heads of Government welcomed the priority given by Commonwealth Health Ministers to the health of women and children in line with international human rights instruments and the MDGs. They encouraged implementation of the Codes of Practice for the International Recruitment of Health Workers, to limit the active recruitment of health workers from vulnerable Commonwealth countries.

79 Heads of Government called for strong regulatory frameworks to combat the manufacture, trade and distribution of counterfeit drugs and stressed the need for access to appropriate drugs at affordable prices.

80 Heads of Government expressed their commitment to take all necessary steps to prevent, prepare for and respond to pandemic threats, including avian influenza. In this context, they welcomed the outcomes of the Ottawa ministerial meeting and other international initiatives.

Education

81 Heads of Government affirmed the centrality of education to development and democracy, as it provides the foundation for realising broader Commonwealth political, economic and social objectives. They commended the efforts of Commonwealth Governments that have successfully invested in the education of their people, encouraged all governments to allocate the resources necessary to meet the education MDGs and noted with appreciation the attainment by some Commonwealth countries of the MDGs on gender equality in primary and secondary education.

82 Heads of Government noted the call by Commonwealth Education Ministers for implementation of the 2004 Protocol for the

Recruitment of Commonwealth teachers and complementary measures, to limit the adverse effects of teacher migration upon the most vulnerable Commonwealth countries.

Gender issues

83 Heads of Government endorsed the new Commonwealth Plan of Action for Gender Equality 2005–15, agreed by Women's Affairs Ministers at their 7th Meeting in the Fiji Islands in June 2004, consistent with the International Conference on Population and Development and the Beijing Declaration and Platform for Action. They supported the call of Women's Affairs Ministers for the allocation of adequate resources to ensure the full and effective implementation of the Plan of Action.

84 Heads of Government welcomed the declaration adopted at the 49th Session of the United Nations Commission on the Status of Women, in particular the unequivocal reaffirmation of the Beijing Declaration and Platform for Action and the outcome of the 23rd Special Session of the United Nations General Assembly, and called for their full and urgent accelerated implementation.

85 Heads of Government acknowledged that gender equality and women's rights are essential preconditions for the achievement of development, MDGs, democracy and peace. They expressed their resolve to achieve political, economic and social equality for women as outlined in the Beijing Platform for Action and international instruments such as the Convention on the Elimination of All Forms of Discrimination against Women (CEDAW), so as to create the necessary environment for the promotion, protection and full realisation of the rights of women and girls.

86 Heads of Government requested the Commonwealth Secretariat to assist member countries in achieving the MDGs on gender equality and women's empowerment, as well as promoting gender equality through the other seven MDGs.

Youth

87 Heads of Government recognised the work of the Commonwealth Youth Programme (CYP) in maximising the participation of young people in development and democracy and in the shaping of their communities. They noted CYP's efforts to address the issues of poverty reduction, HIV/AIDS and capacity-building. Heads of Government also noted the report of the Commonwealth

Youth Forum held from 16–23 November 2005 in Malta and reaffirmed their commitment to the inclusion of youth in Commonwealth efforts that sought achievement of the MDGs.

Sport

88 Heads of Government underlined the important role of sport as an effective instrument for community and youth development in terms of building character, discipline, tolerance and friendship, promoting fair and open sporting competition, protecting the integrity of young athletes and in creating broader opportunities for socio-economic development in the Commonwealth. They acknowledged that the meeting of Commonwealth Sports Ministers in Melbourne on 14 March 2006, before the commencement of the Commonwealth Games, will be an opportunity to strategically develop policies and programmes for the development of youth through sport in the Commonwealth in the context of wider approach to achieving development objectives in health, education and gender equality.

Commonwealth Functional Co-operation

89 Heads of Government noted the various aspects of Commonwealth Functional Cooperation presented to the Committee of the Whole (COW). They appreciated the valuable work of the Commonwealth Secretariat and its partner organisations in implementing CHOGM and CMAG mandates. They requested the Secretary-General to bring to the notice of Heads of Government any proposed mandates arising from ministerial meetings that have significant implications for the Secretariat's work programme and resources. Heads of Government also acknowledged in particular the contribution of the Commonwealth Inter-Governmental Agencies and Commonwealth Organisations which reported to the COW.
90 Heads of Government noted ongoing efforts to strengthen strategic planning, administration, budgeting and evaluation activities and encouraged further work by the Secretariat in these areas.

Civil society

91 Heads of Government acknowledged the contribution of civil society, including in supporting democracy, human rights, peace and development. They also acknowledged that governments and

civil society share a common objective in addressing development and governance challenges and acknowledged the importance of partnership underpinned by sound institutional, legal and policy frameworks. They urged civil society to be proactive in the local and national environment with well-defined priorities and governance arrangements.

92 Heads of Government noted the steps being taken by the Commonwealth and its institutions to mainstream civil society in all activities and called for these efforts to be increased. They noted civil society's call for the Commonwealth to use its international standing to advocate for policy coherence at the global level.

Commonwealth Foundation

93 Heads of Government received the Report of the Commonwealth Foundation and commended its work in enhancing civil society's engagement and dialogue with ministerial meetings, Commonwealth Secretariat programmes and activities, and the COW. They recognised the resulting opportunities for governments and civil society to address development and governance challenges and Commonwealth priorities through joint partnerships. They expressed support for the Foundation's work in building such cooperation, as well as its programmes to strengthen the work of civil society in achieving democracy, sustainable development and cultural understanding in member countries. They also welcomed the Foundation's plans to expand its work through a combination of increased membership, partnerships, and voluntary contributions.

Commonwealth of Learning (COL)

94 In recognition of the challenges facing the higher education sector, Heads of Government requested the COL to assist member countries in further developing expertise in the areas of quality assurance mechanisms for open and distance learning, developing criteria for opening and operating distance learning programmes, accreditation of open and distance learning programmes and undertaking trans-border education. They further encouraged member governments to enhance their contribution, as appropriate, to the budget of COL to enable it to carry out these programmes. Heads of Government also expressed satisfaction with the implementation by COL of Commonwealth Education Ministers' call for

the establishment of a Virtual University for Small States of the Commonwealth.

Commonwealth Business Council (CBC)

95   Heads of Government commended the CBC's work to enhance trade and investment by providing a bridge between the private sector and Governments, between developed and emerging markets, and between large and small businesses. They welcomed the dialogue with the private sector through the Commonwealth Business Forum and requested the CBC to carry forward its work in collaboration with governments.

Commonwealth Partnership for Technology Management (CPTM)

96   Heads of Government welcomed the report of the Commonwealth Secretary-General on the respective roles of and linkages between the CPTM and CBC. They noted the CPTM's networking and partnership dialogues, and also encouraged CPTM to pursue its mandate to promote technology management and exchange in the Commonwealth.

97   Heads of Government also noted the annual international Smart Partnership Dialogues organised by the CPTM on strategic issues, held alternately in Africa and Malaysia. They further commended all Commonwealth countries which have contributed to the CPTM Endowment Fund, as well as all the private sector companies in various Commonwealth countries which have also made important contributions. They encouraged new contributions from other Commonwealth governments and their respective private sectors.

98   Heads of Government decided that the governance arrangements of the CPTM should be changed as proposed by the Secretary-General. They also decided that CPTM should report to the pre-CHOGM meeting of Foreign Ministers on a biennial basis.

Submissions to CHOGM

99   Heads of Government noted the submissions of the Commonwealth of Learning, Commonwealth Foundation, Commonwealth Business Council and civil society representatives, which reported to Foreign Ministers. They also received submissions from the Commonwealth Youth Forum and other Commonwealth civil society organisations which met in Malta on the eve of CHOGM.

100 Heads of Government noted that some of the issues raised in these submissions had been covered in their Communiqué. They requested the Secretary-General to take their recommendations into account, where possible, while implementing CHOGM mandates.

Commonwealth membership

101 Heads of Government received a paper from the Secretary-General on the status of applications for the membership of the Commonwealth. They mandated the Secretary-General to convene a Working Committee at the appropriate political level to consider the issues raised in the paper as well as any other issues which may be relevant to the subject, and to report its findings to the next CHOGM.

Next meeting

102 Heads of Government agreed to meet in Kampala in 2007 at the invitation of the Government of Uganda.
103 They also accepted an offer from the Prime Minister of Trinidad and Tobago to host the 2009 CHOGM.

Malta
27 November 2005

Notes

Introduction

1 Ian Taylor, "Legitimisation and De-legitimisation within a Multilateral Organisation: South Africa and the Commonwealth," *Politikon* 27, no. 1 (2000): 51.

2 See Timothy M. Shaw, "The Commonwealth(s) and Global Governance," *Global Governance* 10, no. 4 (2004): 499–516.

3 On this burgeoning literature, see especially: Margaret Keck and Kathryn Sikkink, *Activists Beyond Borders: advocacy networks in international politics* (Ithaca, N.Y.: Cornell University Press, 1998); Sanjeev Khagram, James Riker and Kathryn Sikkink, eds., *Restructuring World Politics: transnational social movements, networks and norms* (Minneapolis: University of Minnesota Press, 2002); Thomas G. Weiss, "Governance, Good Governance and Global Governance," *Third World Quarterly* 21, no. 5 (2000): 795–814; and Rorden Wilkinson, ed., *The Global Governance Reader* (London: Routledge, 2005).

4 See United Nations, *Our Global Neighbourhood: The Report of the Commission on Global Governance* (New York: Oxford University Press, 1995).

5 The British empire included a diverse range of colonies and protectorates, with India, which included the whole subcontinent of South Asia, always being special. The Dominions of white settlement constituted something of a loose global federation, reinforced by being allies in the Boer then world wars. In the nineteenth century, Australia, Canada, New Zealand and South Africa were "immigrant countries" despite the presence of indigenous communities

6 Despite well established republican and isolationist traditions in the United States, some conservative, mainly white male, groups particularly on the east coast, still dream of special affiliations with a traditional Britain, not recognizing that it has become a very multiracial, multicultural society.

7 Richard Bourne, "The Commonwealth into the 21st Century: new challenges and institutional reform," in *The Commonwealth in the 21st Century*, ed. Greg Mills and John Stremlau (Johannesburg: South African Institute of International Affairs, November 1999), 15.

8 See *inter alia* Diane Stone, ed., *Banking on Knowledge: the genesis of the GDN* (London: Routledge, 2000); and Jean-Phillipe Therien and Vincent

Pouliot, "The Global Compact: shifting the politics of international development?" *Global Governance* 12, no. 1 (2006): 55–75.

9 See Timothy Shaw, "Four Decades of Commonwealth Secretariat and Foundation: continuing contributions to global governance?" *Round Table* 94, no. 310 (July 2005): 359–65.

10 See David Armstrong, "From International Community to International Organisation?" *Commonwealth and Comparative Politics* 39, no. 3 (2001): 31–50.

11 Richard Green, ed., *Commonwealth Yearbook 2005* (Cambridge: Nexus Strategic Partnerships for Commonwealth Secretariat).

12 There is an interesting distinction in the global institutions which are being analyzed in the present series between the majority in which states are the major players and the minority in which non-state actors are more influential. The latter include Elizabeth R. DeSombre, *Global Environmental Institutions* (Abingdon, UK: Routledge, 2006); Geoffrey Allen Pigman, *The World Economic Forum: a multi-stakeholder approach to global governance* (Abingdon, UK: Routledge, 2007); Michael G. Schechter, *UN Global Conferences* (Abingdon, UK: Routledge, 2005); and Peter Willetts, *NGOs in Global Politics* (forthcoming); even Hugo Dobson, *The Group of 7/8* (Abingdon, UK: Routledge, 2007).

13 See Andrew F. Cooper, *Test of Global Governance: Canadian diplomacy and UN world conferences* (Tokyo: UNU Press, 2004); Keck and Sikkink, *Activists beyond Borders*; Robert O'Brien, Anne Marie Goetz, Jan Aart Scholte and Marc Williams, *Contesting Global Governance: multilateral economic institutions and global movements* (Cambridge: Cambridge University Press, 2000); and Weiss, "Governance, Good Governance and Global Governance."

14 Taylor, "Legitimation and De-legitimation within a Multilateral Organisation."

15 The most recent examples in this genre in the new century, both included in the Select Bibliography at the end of this book are: David W. McIntyre, *A Guide to the Contemporary Commonwealth* (London: Palgrave, 2001) and Krishnan Srinivasan, *The Rise, Decline and Future of the British Commonwealth* (London: Palgrave Macmillan, 2005), the latter being the focus of a review section on "Whose Commonwealth?" by five analysts in *Round Table* 96, no. 388 (2007): 57–70.

1 Commonwealth(s)—inter- and non-state

1 Thomas G. Weiss, "Governance, Good Governance and Global Governance," *Third World Quarterly* 21, no. 5 (2000): 810.

2 Deryck Schreuder, "A Commonwealth for the 21st Century: an organization whose time has come?" *Round Table* 91, no. 367 (2002): 652.

3 Richard Bourne, "The Commonwealth into the 21st Century: new challenges and institutional reform," in *The Commonwealth in the 21st Century*, ed. Greg Mills and John Stremlau (Johannesburg: South African Institute of International Affairs, November 1999), 15–16.

4 Greg Mills and John Stremlau, eds., *The Commonwealth in the 21st Century* (Johannesburg: South African Institute of International Affairs, November 1999), 8.

5 David McIntyre, *A Guide to the Contemporary Commonwealth* (London: Palgrave, 2001), 112.

6 See titles already published in the Global Institutions series by Edward C. Luck, M. J. Peterson and James Raymond Vreeland.
7 McIntyre, *A Guide to the Contemporary Commonwealth*, 165.
8 Ibid., 168.
9 Alison Duxbury, "Rejuvenating the Commonwealth: the human rights remedy," *International and Comparative Law Quarterly* 46, no. 2 (1997): 345.
10 See Thomas G. Weiss, Tatiana Carayannis, Richard Jolly, and Louis Emmerij, *UN Voices: the struggle for development and social justice* (Bloomington: Indiana University Press for UNIHP, 2005) and Craig N. Murphy, *The UNDP: a better way?* (Cambridge: Cambridge University Press for UNDP, 2006).
11 See Terry Barringer, *Administering Empire: an annotated checklist of personal memoirs and related studies* (London: Institute of Commonwealth Studies, 2004. Second expanded edition forthcoming in 2007).
12 See Timothy M. Shaw, "The Commonwealth(s)—Inter- and Non-state—at the Start of the Twenty-first Century: contributions to global development/governance," *Third World Quarterly* 24, no. 4 (2003): 729–44 and "Towards 'New Multilateralisms'? Globalization, anti-globalization and the Commonwealth," *Commonwealth and Comparative Politics* 41, no. 3 (2004): 1–12.
13 Peter Vale and David R. Black, "Seizing the Future: post-apartheid South Africa and the 'post-modern' Commonwealth," *Behind the Headlines* 51, no. 4 (1994): 14.
14 McIntyre, *A Guide to the Contemporary Commonwealth*, 77.
15 Krishnan Srinivasan, *The Rise, Decline and Future of the British Commonwealth* (London: Palgrave Macmillan, 2005).
16 Kate Ford and Sunder Katwala, *Reinventing the Commonwealth* (London: Foreign Policy Centre, 1999), 55.
17 Srinivasan, *The Rise, Decline and Future of the British Commonwealth*, 83–106.
18 Ibid., 89.
19 Ibid., 105.
20 Ibid., 94.
21 Ibid., 105.
22 McIntyre, *A Guide to the Contemporary Commonwealth*, 121.
23 UN, *Our Global Neighbourhood: Report of the Commission on Global Governance* (New York: Oxford University Press for UN, 1995) 2–3.
24 Ibid., 6.
25 Margaret Keck and Kathryn Sikkinck, *Activists Beyond Borders* (Ithaca, N.Y.: Cornell University Press, 1998), 9.
26 Mills and Stremlau, *The Commonwealth in the 21st Century*, 11.

2 From decolonization to democratization

1 David McIntyre, *A Guide to the Contemporary Commonwealth* (London: Palgrave, 2001), 27.
2 See ibid., 3.
3 See ibid., 10 and Timothy M. Shaw, "Four Decades of Commonwealth Secretariat and Foundation: continuing contributions to global governance?" *Round Table* 94, no. 380 (2005): 359–65.
4 McIntyre, *A Guide to the Contemporary Commonwealth*, 16.
5 Ibid., 19.

6 See Neta Crawford and Audie Klotz, eds., *How Sanctions Work: lessons from South Africa* (London: Macmillan, 1999).
7 See Timothy M. Shaw, "The Commonwealth(s)—Inter- and Non-state—at the Start of the Twenty-first Century: contributions to global development/governance?" *Third World Quarterly* 24, no. 4 (2003): 729–44, and "Towards 'New Multilateralisms'? Globalization, anti-globalization and the Commonwealth," *Commonwealth and Comparative Politics* 41, no. 3 (2003): 1–12.
8 McIntyre, *A Guide to the Contemporary Commonwealth*, 43.
9 Ibid., 80.

3 Commonwealths today

1 Stephen Chan, "Commonwealth Residualism and the Machinations of Power in a Turbulent Zimbabwe," *Commonwealth and Comparative Politics* 39, no. 3 (2001): 53.
2 See Emeka Anyaoku, *The Inside Story of the Modern Commonwealth* (London: Evans, 2004).
3 See Andrew F. Cooper, *Celebrity Diplomacy* (Boulder, Col.: Paradigm, forthcoming).
4 See Ramesh Thakur, Andrew F. Cooper and John English, eds., *International Commissions and the Power of Ideas* (Tokyo: UNU Press, 2005).
5 See Commonwealth Foundation, "Citizens and Governance: civil society in the new millennium" (London, March 2001).
6 Commonwealth Foundation 2004.
7 Commonwealth Foundation, "Report of the Commonwealth Civil Society Meeting on Development and Democracy, Abuja, Nigeria, December 2003" (London, 2004), 47.
8 David Armstrong, "From International Community to International Organization?" *Commonwealth and Comparative Politics* 39, no. 3 (2001): 44 and 47.
9 "Foreword from the President," *Learning for Development: Three-year Plan, 2006–2009* (Vancouver: COL, 2006), 6.
10 See Kate Ford and Sunder Katwala, *Reinventing the Commonwealth* (London: Foreign Policy Centre, 1999), 10.
11 See David McIntyre, *A Guide to the Contemporary Commonwealth* (London: Palgrave, 2001), 169–70.
12 Ibid., 189.
13 See ibid., 65, 130 and 155–60.
14 Ibid., 160.
15 For a useful tabular chronology of how a democratic Commonwealth evolved, see Ford and Katwala, *Reinventing the Commonwealth*, 23.
16 See Amanda Sives, "Election Observation and Deepening Democracy in the Commonwealth," *Round Table* 90, no. 361 (2001): 507–28.
17 *Directory of Commonwealth Scholars and Fellows 1960–2002* (London: ACU, 2003).
18 See Stephen Fletcher, "Poor Commonwealth no Longer? Challenges to the Commonwealth in Achieving UN MDGs" (London and Windsor, UK: Commonwealth Secretariat, Cumberland Lodge and Goodenough College, 2006).

150 *Notes*

19 See David McIntyre, Stuart Mole, Lucian M. Ashworth, Timothy M. Shaw, and Alex May, "Whose Commonwealth? Responses to Krishnan Srinivasan's *The Rise, Decline and Future of the British Commonwealth*," *Round Table* 96, no. 388 (2007): 57–70.
20 See Vicky Randall, ed., "Special Issue on the Commonwealth in Comparative Perspective," *Commonwealth and Comparative Politics* 39, no. 3 (2001): 1–164.

4 Commonwealths' discourses and directions

1 David Armstrong, "From International Community to International Organization?" *Commonwealth and Comparative Politics* 39, no. 3 (2001): 46.
2 Ruth Lea, "The Best Club on the Planet," *Commonwealth Press Quarterly* (April 2006): 8.
3 Jan Aart Scholte, *Globalization: a critical introduction* (London: Palgrave Macmillan, 2005. Second edition), 22.
4 Ibid., 209.
5 Marlies Glasius, Mary Kaldor and Helmut Anheier, eds., *Global Civil Society 2002* (Oxford: Oxford University Press for the LSE, 2002), 3.
6 Armstrong, "From International Community to International Organization?" 43.
7 See Scholte, *Globalization: a critical introduction*, 396–423.
8 Krishnan Srinivasan, *The Rise, Decline and Future of the British Commonwealth* (London: Palgrave Macmillan, 2005), 138.
9 World Bank, *Global Economic Prospects 2006: economic implications of remittances and migration* (Washington D.C., 2006), 85–87.
10 Ibid., 89.
11 Paul Sutton, "Small States and the Commonwealth," *Commonwealth and Comparative Politics* 39, no. 3 (2001): 75.
12 David McIntyre, *A Guide to the Contemporary Commonwealth* (London: Palgrave, 2001), 117.
13 Sutton, *Globalization: a critical introduction,* 75.
14 Ibid., 81.
15 See ibid., 89.
16 Anthony Payne, "Small States and the Global Politics of Development," *Round Table* 93, no. 376 (2004): 634.
17 Commonwealth Secretariat, "Learning from Each Other: Commonwealth Studies for the Twenty-first Century" (London, June 1996): 15.
18 Ibid., 16.
19 Anthony Payne, "Resetting the Table for Commonwealth Studies at the Beginning of the Twenty-first Century," *Round Table* 91, no. 367 (2002): 658.
20 Ibid., 661.
21 Payne, "Small States and the Global Politics of Development," 623.
22 Anthony Payne, *Global Politics of Unequal Development* (London: Palgrave Macmillan, 2005), 245–47.
23 Ibid., 45.
24 See Andrew F. Cooper, Agata Antkiewicz and Timothy M. Shaw "Economic Size Trumps all Else? Lessons from BRICSAM" (Waterloo, Ontario: CIGI, December 2006. Working Paper #12. www.cigionline.org).
25 See Naomi Klein, *No Logo* (New York: Picador, 2000) and www.nologo.org

26 See ibid., 227–29.
27 See Jean-Philippe Therien and Vincent Pouliot, "The Global Compact: shifting the politics of international development," *Global Governance* 12, no. 1 (2006): 55–75.

5 Commonwealths and the competition

1 Vicky Randall, "Introduction: the meaning of the Commonwealth today. Special Issue on the Commonwealth in Comparative Perspective," *Commonwealth and Comparative Politics* 39, no. 3 (2001): 5.
2 David Crystal, *The English Language: a guided tour of the language* (London: Penguin, Second edition), 280–81.
3 David Graddol, "English Next" (London: British Council), 12 and 13.
4 See Thomas G. Weiss, Tatiana Carayannis, Richard Jolly, and Louis Emmerij, *UN Voices: the struggle for development and social justice* (Bloomington: Indiana University Press for UNIHP, 2005).
5 Randall, "The Meaning of the Commonwealth today," 4.
6 David McIntyre, *A Guide to the Contemporary Commonwealth* (London: Palgrave, 2001): 201.
7 Randall, "The Meaning of the Commonwealth today," 1.

6 Commonwealths and the future

1 David McIntyre, *A Guide to the Contemporary Commonwealth* (London: Palgrave, 2001), 221.
2 John Stremlau, "The Commonwealth: contributing to civility on the eve of the citizen century," in *The Commonwealth in the 21st Century*, ed. Greg Mills and John Stremlau (Johannesburg: SAIIA, November 1999), 65.
3 Commonwealth Secretariat, "Making Democracy Work for Pro-poor Development: report by a Commonwealth Expert Group" (London, October 2003), ix.
4 Ibid., 69.
5 Ibid., 67–68 and xv.
6 Ibid., 68 and ix.
7 Stremlau, "The Commonwealth," 63.
8 Stephen Chan, "Commonwealth Residualism and the Machinations of Power in a Turbulent Zimbabwe," *Commonwealth and Comparative Politics* 39, no. 3 (2001): 52.
9 David Armstrong, "From International Community to International Organization?" *Commonwealth and Comparative Politics* 39, no. 3 (2001): 47.
10 See David McIntyre, Stuart Mole, Lucian M. Ashworth, Timothy M. Shaw, and Alex May, "Whose Commonwealth? Responses to Krishnan Srinivasan's *The Rise, Decline and Future of the British Commonwealth*," *Round Table* 96, no. 388 (2007): 65–78.
11 See Jean-Philippe Therien, "Beyond the North-South Divide: the two tales of world poverty," *Third World Quarterly* 20, no. 4 (1999): 723–42.
12 House of Commons, "The Future of the Commonwealth: Report of the Foreign Affairs Committee" (London: HMSO, March 1996), 12.
13 See Rob Jenkins, "Reassessing the Commonwealth" (London: RIIA with CPA and ICS. Discussion Paper no. 72).

14 Kate Ford and Sunder Katwala, *Reinventing the Commonwealth* (London: Foreign Policy Centre, 1999), 38.
15 McIntyre, *A Guide to the Contemporary Commonwealth,* 221.
16 Ibid., 229.
17 Ibid., 227.
18 See *inter alia* Thomas G. Weiss, Tatiana Carayannis, Richard Jolly, and Louis Emmerij, *UN Voices: the struggle for development and social justice* (Bloomington: Indiana University Press for UNIHP, 2005) and Craig N. Murphy, *The UNDP: a better way?* (Cambridge: Cambridge University Press for UNDP, 2006).
19 See *inter alia* Inderjeet Parmar, *Think Tanks and Power in Foreign Policy* (London: Palgrave, 2004) and Diane Stone and Simon Maxwell, eds., *Global Knowledge Networks and International Development* (London: Routledge, 2004).
20 Geoffrey Allen Pigman, *The World Economic Forum: a multi-stakeholder approach to global governance* (Abingdon, UK: Routledge, 2007. Global Institutions series), 55.
21 See Douglas Lemke, "African Lessons for International Relations Research," *World Politics* 56, no. 1 (2003): 114–38 and William Brown, "Africa and International Relations: a comment on IR theory," *Review of International Studies* 32, no. 1 (2006): 119–43.

Select bibliography

Emeka Anyaoku, *The Inside Story of the Modern Commonwealth* (London: Evans, 2004). A comprehensive autobiography of the third secretary-general (see also Box 3.1) with a focus on Commonwealth Secretariat diplomacy around apartheid and norms for democratic governance.

Commonwealth Ministers Reference Book 2006 (London: Henley Media for Commonwealth Secretariat, 2006). Comprehensive guide to the official view and role of the intergovernmental Commonwealth and its member states.

Commonwealth Scholarship and Fellowship Programme, *Directory of Commonwealth Scholars and Fellows 1960–2002* (London: ACU, 2003). Who's who of Commonwealth scholars over the last half century; invaluable listing of post-independence national and regional leaders.

Commonwealth Secretariat, "Making Democracy Work for Pro-poor Development: report by a Commonwealth Expert Group" (London, October 2003). The "Manmohan Singh report" which presents an informed, consensual overview of the state of the debate in the Commonwealths about steps toward development and democracy with reference to the MDGs.

Richard Green, ed., *Commonwealth Yearbook 2006* (Cambridge: Nexus Strategic Partnerships for Commonwealth Secretariat, 2006). Latest annual Marlborough House perspectives, non- as well as inter-state, on current Commonwealth issues with contributions from major ComSec officers and others.

David W. McIntyre, *A Guide to the Contemporary Commonwealth* (London: Palgrave, 2001). Invaluable, current historical encyclopedia by a leading New Zealand scholar; very informed and balanced; a goldmine for other analysts.

Greg Mills and John Stremlau, eds., *The Commonwealth in the 21st Century* (Johannesburg: South African Institute of International Affairs, November 1999). Largely "Southern" perspectives by eight analysts from around the Commonwealth on contemporary Commonwealth issues, from human rights and possibilities of cosmopolitanism to emerging markets and sustainable ecologies.

Vicky Randall, ed., "Special Issue on the Commonwealth in Comparative Perspective," *Commonwealth and Comparative Politics* 39, no. 3 (2001): 1–164. Comprehensive, analytic overview informed by international relations and international organization approaches, which reflects perspectives from the South and North, small and large.

Krishnan Srinivasan, *The Rise, Decline and Future of the British Commonwealth* (London: Palgrave Macmillan, 2005). A rather controversial, idiosyncratic essay on the failures of the British empire, including Britain's disinterest in the contemporary institution, which led to a special section in *Round Table* in February 2007 in which five analysts commented from around the Commonwealth.

Select websites
Websites relevant to intra- and extra-Commonwealths

Inter-state Commonwealths

www.chogm2005.mt
www.chogm2007.ug
www.commonwealthfoundation.com
www.thecommonwealth.org

(NB: A comprehensive list of Commonwealth Secretariat websites can be found in Richard Green, ed., *The Commonwealth Yearbook 2006*, at 38.)

Non-state Commonwealths

www.acu.ac.uk
www1.cata.ca/commonwealth
www.cba.org.uk
www.cbcglobelink.org
www.cjaweb.com
www.clgf.org.uk
www.col.org
www.commonwealthday.com
www.cpahq.org
www.cpu.org.uk
www.csfp-online.org
www.cto.int
www.cumberlandlodge.ac.uk
www.cwgdelhi2010.com
www.humanrightsinitiative.org
www.melbourne2006.com
www.ospa.org.uk
www.rcsint.org
www.thecgf.com

(NB: A comprehensive list of Commonwealth Organizations' websites can be found in Richard Green, ed., *The Commonwealth Yearbook 2006*, at 475–94.)

Commonwealth "Plus"

www.akdn.org
www.antislavery.org
www.attac.org
www.britishcouncil.org
www.cabi.org
www.cba.org.uk
www.cigionline.org
www.civicus.org
www.commonwealth.sas.ac.uk
www.commonwealtheducation.org
www.devstud.org.uk
www.dfid.gov.uk
www.eitrasparency.org
www.en.wikipedia.org/wiki/Commonwealth_of_Nations
www.esu.org
www.foreignpolicy.com
www.formfed.org
www.francophonie.org
www.gdnet.org
www.globalstudiesassociation.org
www.goodenough.ac.uk
http://gstudynet.com
www.halifaxinitiative.org
www.humansecurity.org
www.icbl.org
www.icc-cricket.com
www.indymedia.org
www.moneygram.com
www.moneymart.com
www.nologo.org
www.oneworldtrust.org
www.oxfam.org
www.pacweb.net
www.publishwhatyoupay.org
www.rhodeshouse.ac.uk
www.rugbyworldcup.com
www.sendmoneyhome.org
www.sids.org
www.sidsnet.org/aosis
www.sivglobal.org
www.tandf.co.uk/journals
www.thebackpacker.net
www.twnside.org.sg
www.unglobalcompact.org
www.westernunion.com
www.worldbank.org

Index